811
AMP

CPS – HUBBARD HIGH SCHOOL

Bloom's how to write about Edgar Allan

31670030007556

W9-CKL-549

DATE	ISSUED TO
3-4-15	JOSE RIOZ
MAR 1 7 2015	
	Kevin Capilla
APR 0 4 2017	

© DEMCO 32-2125

BLOOM'S

HOW TO WRITE ABOUT

Edgar Allan Poe

SUSAN AMPER

HUBBARD HIGH SCHOOL LIBRARY
6200 South Hamlin Avenue
Chicago, Illinois 60629

BLOOM'S
LITERARY CRITICISM
An imprint of Infobase Publishing

811
AMP
31670030007556

Bloom's How to Write about Edgar Allan Poe

Copyright © 2008 by Susan Amper

All rights reserved. No part of this book may be reproduced or utilized in any form or by any means, electronic or mechanical, including photocopying, recording, or by any information storage or retrieval systems, without permission in writing from the publisher. For information contact:

Bloom's Literary Criticism
An imprint of Infobase Publishing
132 West 31st Street
New York NY 10001

Library of Congress Cataloging-in-Publication Data

Amper, Susan.
Bloom's how to write about Edgar Allan Poe/Susan Amper; introduction by Harold Bloom.
    p. cm.
  Includes bibliographical references and index.
  ISBN 978-0-7910-9488-4 (alk. paper)
   1. Poe, Edgar Allan, 1809–1849—Criticism and interpretation. 2. Criticism—Authorship. 3. Report writing. I. Bloom, Harold. II. Title. III. Title: How to write about Edgar Allan Poe.

  PS2638.A555 2007
  811'.3—dc22
                              2007008120

Bloom's Literary Criticism books are available at special discounts when purchased in bulk quantities for businesses, associations, institutions, or sales promotions. Please call our Special Sales Department in New York at (212) 967-8800 or (800) 322-8755.

You can find Bloom's Literary Criticism on the World Wide Web
at http://www.chelseahouse.com

Text design by Annie O'Donnell
Cover design by Ben Peterson

Printed in the United States of America

Bang MSRF 10 9 8 7 6 5 4 3 2 1

This book is printed on acid-free paper.

CONTENTS

SERIES
INTRODUCTION

BLOOM'S How to Write about Literature series is designed to inspire students to write fine essays on great writers and their works. Each volume in the series begins with an introduction by Harold Bloom, meditating on the challenges and rewards of writing about the volume's subject author. The first chapter then provides detailed instructions on how to write a good essay, including how to find a thesis; how to develop an outline; how to write a good introduction, body text, and conclusions; how to cite sources; and more. The second chapter provides a brief overview of the issues involved in writing about the subject author and then a number of suggestions for paper topics, with accompanying strategies for addressing each topic. Succeeding chapters cover the author's major works.

The paper topics suggested within this book are open-ended, and the brief strategies provided are designed to give students a push forward on the writing process rather than a roadmap to success. The aim of the book is to pose questions, not answer them. Many different kinds of papers could result from each topic. As always, the success of each paper will depend completely on the writer's skill and imagination.

INTRODUCTION

by Harold Bloom

ONLY A handful of classical American writers are now read world-wide, whether in translation or in the original. They include Poe, Walt Whitman, Mark Twain, William Faulkner, and perhaps T. S. Eliot. Poe's styles have been exalted by Charles-Pierre Baudelaire, Stéphane Mallarmé, and Paul Valéry, none of whom had much of an inner ear for English. Jorge Luis Borges, much affected by Poe's invention of the analytic detective story, spoke and read English as a child, which may be why he admired his precursor's ingenuity but refrained from any comments on Poe's diction.

The first principle in writing about Poe is never to discuss how badly he performed in both prose and verse. Telling the truth about "the jingle man," as Ralph Waldo Emerson termed him, is to invite endless abuse from his army of admirers. In my long experience as a literary critic, I have become hardened and do not read attacks upon me, since I have little time to waste. But I find it worth remarking that only the hordes of J. K. Rowling and Stephen King fans are as intemperate in defense of their idols as is the Poe Society.

So do not even mention Poe's language, metric, or prose rhythms when you desire or need to write about him. At my age I have become irenic and avoid all quarrels. If you must comment on Poe's work, start with his perpetual popularity. Doubtless that will continue forever, unlike the fame of Rowling and of King, whose books will be rubbed away by time as all Period Pieces must be.

Poe is permanent and inescapable. His Gothic tales do not sustain being read aloud, but like his novel, *Arthur Gordon Pym,* they dream universal nightmares. As for his poems, I once granted them the negative distinction of being the very worst written by an American, but the floods of politically correct effusions that have deluged us far transcend Poe's aesthetic badness. At least "The Raven," "The Bells," "Ulalume," "For Annie," and the other famous incantations are written in verse, though they are all paced like a metronome.

I return to the only advice I am capable of giving here: Write about Poe by finding reasons for his enormous popularity. If his appeal were only to the subliterate, it would by now be over. Experience refutes my desire to exclude him from the Canon. G. K. Chesterton and Borges, like Sir Arthur Conan Doyle before them, owed to Poe the invention of the analytic detective story. W. H. Auden celebrated *Eureka*, Poe's long, apocalyptic prose poem, and Richard Wilbur, another distinguished poet and prosodist, defended Poe's lyricism. My own favorite poet, Hart Crane, invokes Poe in "The Tunnel," a subway descent into Hell that helps darken the finest American epic of the 20th century, *The Bridge* (1930).

I still resort to French and German translations when I am compelled to read Poe's tales, and I avoid the poems. Am I wrong? Poe liked to quote the superb English graphic artist William Hogarth, who said that genius was "but *diligence* after all," and Poe certainly was diligent.

In writing about Poe you need *not* share my unhappy concern with his flaws in diction, and even I must testify to his cognitive sophistication. Whether or not I am right about his inadequacies as a stylist, I, too, am impressed that Poe's intercontinental popularity transcends his limitations. My own best advice to those who desire to read, meditate, and then comment upon him is to confront his universality and so begin the enterprise.

HOW TO WRITE
A GOOD ESSAY

WHILE THERE are many ways to write about literature, most assignments for high school and college English classes call for analytical papers. In these assignments, you are presenting your interpretation of a text to your reader. Your objective is to interpret the text's meaning in order to enhance your reader's understanding and enjoyment of the work. Without exception, strong papers about the meaning of a literary work are built upon a careful, close reading of the text or texts. Careful, analytical reading should always be the first step in your writing process. This volume provides models of such reading, and these should help you develop your own skills as a reader and as a writer.

As the examples throughout this book demonstrate, attentive reading entails thinking about and evaluating the formal (textual) aspects of the author's works: theme, character, form, and language. In addition, when writing about a work, many readers choose to move beyond the text itself to consider the work's cultural context. In these instances, writers might explore the historical circumstances of the time period in which the work was written. Alternatively, they might examine the philosophies and ideas that a work addresses. Even in cases where writers explore a work's cultural context, though, papers must still address the more formal aspects of the work itself. A good interpretative essay that evaluates Charles Dickens's use of the philosophy of utilitarianism in his novel *Hard Times,* for example, cannot adequately address the author's treatment of the philosophy without firmly grounding this discussion in the book itself. In other words, any analytical paper about a text, even one that seeks to evaluate the work's cultural context, must also have a

1

firm handle on the work's themes, characters, and language. You must look for and evaluate these aspects of a work, then, as you read a text and as you prepare to write about it.

WRITING ABOUT THEMES

Literary themes are more than just topics or subjects treated in a work; they are attitudes or points about these topics that often structure other elements in a work. Writing about theme therefore requires that you not just identify a topic that a literary work addresses but also discuss what that work says about that topic. For example, if you were writing about the culture of the American South in William Faulkner's famous story "A Rose for Emily," you would need to discuss what Faulkner says, argues, or implies about that culture and its passing.

When you prepare to write about thematic concerns in a work of literature, you will probably discover that, like most works of literature, your text touches upon other themes in addition to its central theme. These secondary themes also provide rich ground for paper topics. A thematic paper on "A Rose for Emily" might consider gender or race in the story. While neither of these could be said to be the central theme of the story, they are clearly related to the passing of the "old South" and could provide plenty of good material for papers.

As you prepare to write about themes in literature, you might find a number of strategies helpful. After you identify a theme or themes in the story, you should begin by evaluating how other elements of the story—such as character, point of view, imagery, and symbolism—help develop the theme. You might ask yourself what your own responses are to the author's treatment of the subject matter. Do not neglect the obvious, either: What expectations does the title set up? How does the title help develop thematic concerns? Clearly, the title "A Rose for Emily" says something about the narrator's attitude toward the title character, Emily Grierson, and all she represents.

WRITING ABOUT CHARACTER

Generally, characters are essential components of fiction and drama. (This is not always the case, though; Ray Bradbury's "August 2026: There

Will Come Soft Rains" is technically a story without characters, at least any human characters.) Often, you can discuss character in poetry, as in T. S. Eliot's "The Love Song of J. Alfred Prufrock" or Robert Browning's "My Last Duchess." Many writers find that analyzing character is one of the most interesting and engaging ways to work with a piece of literature and to shape a paper. After all, characters generally are human, and we all know something about being human and living in the world. While it is always important to remember that these figures are not real people but creations of the writer's imagination, it can be fruitful to begin evaluating them as you might evaluate a real person. Often you can start with your own response to a character. Did you like or dislike the character? Did you sympathize with the character? Why or why not?

Keep in mind, though, that emotional responses like these are just starting places. To truly explore and evaluate literary characters, you need to return to the formal aspects of the text and evaluate how the author has drawn these characters. The 20th-century writer E. M. Forster coined the terms *flat characters* and *round characters*. Flat characters are static, one-dimensional characters who frequently represent a particular concept or idea. In contrast, round characters are fully drawn and much more realistic characters who frequently change and develop over the course of a work. Are the characters you are studying flat or round? What elements of the characters lead you to this conclusion? Why might the author have drawn characters like this? How does their development affect the meaning of the work? Similarly, you should explore the techniques the author uses to develop characters. Do we hear a character's own words, or do we hear only other characters' assessments of him or her? Or does the author use an omniscient or limited omniscient narrator to allow us access to the workings of the character's mind? If so, how does that help develop the characterization? Often you can even evaluate the narrator as a character. How trustworthy are the opinions and assessments of the narrator? You should also think about characters' names. Do they mean anything? If you encounter a heroine named Sophia or Sophie, you should probably think about her wisdom (or lack thereof), since *sophia* means "wisdom" in Greek. Similarly, since the name *Sylvia* is derived from the word *sylvan,* meaning "of the wood," you might want to evaluate that character's relationship with nature. Once again, you might look to the title of the work. Does Herman Melville's "Bartleby the Scrivener" signal anything about Bartleby himself? Is Bartleby adequately defined by his job as scrivener? Is this part of Melville's point? Pursuing questions like these can help you develop thorough papers about characters from psychological, sociological, or more formalistic perspectives.

WRITING ABOUT FORM AND GENRE

Genre, a word derived from French, means "type" or "class." Literary genres are distinctive classes or categories of literary composition. On the most general level, literary works can be divided into the genres of drama, poetry, fiction, and essays, yet within those genres there are classifications that are also referred to as genres. Tragedy and comedy, for example, are genres of drama. Epic, lyric, and pastoral are genres of poetry. *Form*, on the other hand, generally refers to the shape or structure of a work. There are many clearly defined forms of poetry that follow specific patterns of meter, rhyme, and stanza. Sonnets, for example, are poems that follow a fixed form of 14 lines. Sonnets generally follow one of two basic sonnet forms, each with its own distinct rhyme scheme. Haiku is another example of poetic form, traditionally consisting of three unrhymed lines of five, seven, and five syllables.

While you might think that writing about form or genre might leave little room for argument, many of these forms and genres are very fluid. Remember that literature is evolving and ever changing, and so are its forms. As you study poetry, you may find that poets, especially more modern poets, play with traditional poetic forms, bringing about new effects. Similarly, dramatic tragedy was once quite narrowly defined, but over the centuries playwrights have broadened and challenged traditional definitions, changing the shape of tragedy. When Arthur Miller wrote *Death of a Salesman*, many critics challenged the idea that tragic drama could encompass a common man like Willy Loman.

Evaluating how a work of literature fits into or challenges the boundaries of its form or genre can provide you with fruitful avenues of investigation. You might find it helpful to ask why the work does or does not fit into traditional categories. Why might Miller have thought it fitting to write a tragedy of the common man? Similarly, you might compare the content or theme of a work with its form. How well do they work together? Many of Emily Dickinson's poems, for instance, follow the meter of traditional hymns. While some of her poems seem to express traditional religious doctrines, many seem to challenge or strain against traditional conceptions of God and theology. What is the effect, then, of her use of traditional hymn meter?

WRITING ABOUT LANGUAGE, SYMBOLS, AND IMAGERY

No matter what the genre, writers use words as their most basic tool. Language is the most fundamental building block of literature. It is essential that you pay careful attention to the author's language and word choice as you read, reread, and analyze a text. Imagery is language that appeals to the senses. Most commonly, imagery appeals to our sense of vision, creating a mental picture, but authors also use language that appeals to our other senses. Images can be literal or figurative. Literal images use sensory language to describe an actual thing. In the broadest terms, figurative language uses one thing to speak about something else. For example, if I call my boss a snake, I am not saying that he is literally a reptile. Instead, I am using figurative language to communicate my opinions about him. Since we think of snakes as sneaky, slimy, and sinister, I am using the concrete image of a snake to communicate these abstract opinions and impressions.

The two most common figures of speech are similes and metaphors. Both are comparisons between two apparently dissimilar things. Similes are explicit comparisons using the words *like* or *as*; and metaphors are implicit comparisons. To return to the previous example, if I say, "My boss, Bob, was waiting for me when I showed up to work five minutes late today—the snake!" I have constructed a metaphor. Writing about his experiences fighting in World War I, Wilfred Owen begins his poem "Dulce et decorum est" with a string of similes: "Bent double, like old beggars under sacks, / Knock-kneed, coughing like hags, we cursed through sludge." Owen's goal was to undercut clichéd notions that war and dying in battle were glorious. Certainly, comparing soldiers to coughing hags and to beggars underscores his point.

"Fog," a short poem by Carl Sandburg, provides a clear example of a metaphor. Sandburg's poem reads:

The fog comes
on little cat feet.

It sits looking
over harbor and city
on silent haunches
and then moves on.

Notice how effectively Sandburg conveys surprising impressions of the fog by comparing two seemingly disparate things—the fog and a cat.

Symbols, by contrast, are things that stand for, or represent, other things. Often they represent something intangible, such as concepts or ideas. In everyday life we use and understand symbols easily. Babies at christenings and brides at weddings wear white to represent purity. Think, too, of a dollar bill. The paper itself has no value in and of itself. Instead, that paper bill is a symbol of something else, the precious metal in a nation's coffers. Symbols in literature work similarly. Authors use symbols to evoke more than a simple, straightforward, literal meaning. Characters, objects, and places can all function as symbols. Famous literary examples of symbols include Moby-Dick, the white whale of Herman Melville's novel, and the scarlet *A* of Nathaniel Hawthorne's *The Scarlet Letter.* As both of these symbols suggest, a literary symbol cannot be adequately defined or explained by any one meaning. Hester Prynne's Puritan community clearly intends her scarlet *A* as a symbol of her adultery, but as the novel progresses, even her own community reads the letter as representing not just *adultery,* but *able, angel,* and a host of other meanings.

Writing about imagery and symbols requires close attention to the author's language. To prepare a paper on symbolism or imagery in a work, identify and trace the images and symbols and then try to draw some conclusions about how they function. Ask yourself how any symbols or images help contribute to the themes or meanings of the work. What connotations do they carry? How do they affect your reception of the work? Do they shed light on characters or settings? A strong paper on imagery or symbolism will thoroughly consider the use of figures in the text and will try to reach some conclusions about how or why the author uses them.

WRITING ABOUT HISTORY AND CONTEXT

As noted above, it is possible to write an analytical paper that also considers the work's context. After all, the text was not created in a vacuum. The author lived and wrote in a specific time period and in a specific cultural context and, like all of us, was shaped by that environment. Learning more about the historical and cultural circumstances that surround the author and the work can help illuminate a text and provide you with productive material for a paper. Remember, though, that when you write analytical papers, you should use the context to illuminate the text. Do not lose sight of your goal—to interpret the meaning of the literary work. Use historical or philosophical research as a tool to develop your textual evaluation.

Thoughtful readers often consider how history and culture affected the author's choice and treatment of his or her subject matter. Investigations into the history and context of a work could examine the work's relation to specific historical events, such as the Salem witch trials in 17th-century Massachusetts or the restoration of Charles to the British throne in 1660. Bear in mind that historical context is not limited to politics and world events. While knowing about the Vietnam War is certainly helpful in interpreting much of Tim O'Brien's fiction, and some knowledge of the French Revolution clearly illuminates the dynamics of Charles Dickens's *A Tale of Two Cities*, historical context also entails the fabric of daily life. Examining a text in light of gender roles, race relations, class boundaries, or working conditions can give rise to thoughtful and compelling papers. Exploring the conditions of the working class in 19th-century England, for example, can provide a particularly effective avenue for writing about Dickens's *Hard Times*.

You can begin thinking about these issues by asking broad questions at first. What do you know about the time period and about the author? What does the editorial apparatus in your text tell you? These might be starting places. Similarly, when specific historical events or dynamics are particularly important to understanding a work but might be somewhat obscure to modern readers, textbooks usually provide notes to explain historical background. These make a good place to start. With this information, ask yourself how these historical facts and circumstances might have affected the author, the presentation of theme, and the presentation of character. How does knowing more about the work's specific historical context illuminate the work? To take a well-known example, understanding the complex attitudes toward slavery during the time Mark Twain wrote *The Adventures of Huckleberry Finn* should help you begin to examine issues of race in the text. Additionally, you might compare these attitudes to those of the time in which the novel was set. How might this comparison affect your interpretation of a work written after the abolition of slavery but set before the Civil War?

WRITING ABOUT PHILOSOPHY AND IDEAS

Philosophical concerns are closely related to both historical context and thematic issues. Like historical investigation, philosophical research can provide a useful tool as you analyze a text. For example, an investigation into the working class in Dickens's England might lead you to a topic on the philosophical doctrine of utilitarianism in *Hard Times.* Many other works explore philosophies and ideas quite explicitly. Mary Shelley's famous novel *Frankenstein,* for example, explores John Locke's tabula rasa theory of human knowledge as it portrays the intellectual and emotional development of Victor Frankenstein's creature. As this example indicates, philosophical issues are somewhat more abstract than investigations of theme or historical context. Some other examples of philosophical issues include human free will, the formation of human identity, the nature of sin, or questions of ethics.

Writing about philosophy and ideas might require some outside research, but usually the notes or other material in your text will provide you with basic information and often footnotes and bibliographies suggest places you can go to read further about the subject. If you have identified a philosophical theme that runs through a text, you might ask yourself how the author develops this theme. Look, for example, at character development and the interactions of characters. You might also examine whether the narrative voice in a work of fiction addresses the philosophical concerns of the text.

WRITING COMPARE AND CONTRAST ESSAYS

Finally, you might find that comparing and contrasting the works or techniques of an author provides a useful tool for literary analysis. A compare and contrast essay might compare two characters or themes in a single work, or it might compare the author's treatment of a theme in two works. It might also contrast methods of character development or analyze an author's differing treatment of a philosophical concern in two works. Writing compare and contrast essays, though, requires some special consideration. While they generally provide you with plenty of material to use, they also come with a built-in trap: the laundry list. Papers often become mere lists of connections between the works. As this chapter will discuss, a strong thesis must make an assertion that you want to prove or validate. A strong compare/contrast thesis, then, needs to comment on the significance of the similarities and differences you observe. It is not enough merely to assert that the works contain similarities and differences. You might, for example, state why the similarities and differences are important and explain how they illuminate the works' treatment of theme. Remember, too, that a thesis should not be a statement of the obvious. A compare/contrast paper that focuses only on very obvious similarities or differences does little to illuminate the connections between the works. Often, an effective method of shaping a strong thesis and argument is to begin your paper by noting the similarities between the works but then to develop a thesis that asserts how these apparently similar elements are different. If, for example, you observe that Walt Whitman wrote a number of poems using the image of grass, you might analyze how he uses grass imagery differently in two poems. Similarly, many scholars have noted that Poe created many psychologically troubled characters who are haunted by doppelgangers. A good thesis comparing two of these characters—William Wilson of "William Wilson" and the narrator of "The Tell-Tale Heart," for example—might initially identify both characters as examples of Poe's psychologically troubled type but then argue whether each narrator's doppelganger is real or imaginary? Are the events real or imagined? Is each tale just an allegory, or can the events be read as actually occurring? If you strive to analyze the similarities or differences, discuss significances, and avoid the obvious, your paper should avoid the laundry-list trap.

PREPARING TO WRITE

Armed with a clear sense of your task—illuminating the text—and with an understanding of theme, character, language, history, and philosophy, you are ready to approach the writing process. Remember that good writing is grounded in good reading and that close reading takes time, attention, and more than one reading of your text. Read for comprehension first. As you go back and review the work, mark the text to chart the details of the work as well as your reactions. Highlight important passages, repeated words, and image patterns. "Converse" with the text through marginal notes. Mark turns in the plot, ask questions, and make observations about characters, themes, and language. If you are reading from a book that does not belong to you, keep a record of your reactions in a journal or notebook. If you have read a work of literature carefully, paying attention to both the text and the context of the work, you have a leg up on the writing process. Admittedly, at this point, your ideas are probably very broad and undefined, but you have taken an important first step toward writing a strong paper.

Your next step is to focus, to take a broad or fuzzy topic and define it more clearly. Even a topic provided by your instructor will need to be focused appropriately. Remember that good writers make the topic their own. There are a number of strategies that you can use to develop your own focus. In one such strategy, *freewriting*, you spend 10 minutes or so just writing about your topic without referring back to the text or your notes. Write whatever comes to mind; the important thing is that you just keep writing. Often this process allows you to develop fresh ideas or approaches to your subject matter. You could also try *brainstorming*: Write down your topic and then list all the related points or ideas you can think of. Include questions, comments, words, important passages or events, and anything else that comes to mind. Let one idea lead to another. In the related technique of *clustering*, or *mapping*, you write your topic on a sheet of paper and write related ideas around it. Then list related subpoints under each of these main ideas. Many people then draw arrows to show connections between points. This technique helps you narrow your topic and can also help you organize your ideas. Similarly, asking journalistic questions—Who? What? Where? When? Why? and How?—can develop ideas for topic development.

Thesis Statements

Once you have developed a focused topic, you can begin to think about your thesis statement, the main point of your paper. It is imperative that you craft a strong thesis; otherwise, your paper will likely be little more than random, disorganized observations about the text. Think of your thesis statement as a kind of road map for your paper. It tells your reader where you are going and how you are going to get there.

To craft a good thesis, you must keep a number of things in mind. First, as the title of this subsection indicates, your paper's thesis should be a statement, an assertion about the text that you want to prove or validate. Beginning writers often formulate a question that they attempt to use as a thesis. For example, a writer exploring the theme of guilt in Poe's "The Tell-Tale Heart" might ask, What ideas does the story raise about the narrator's guilt, and what attitudes toward his guilt does the story engender in the reader? While a question like this is a good strategy to use in the invention process to help narrow your topic and find your thesis, it cannot serve as the thesis statement because it does not tell your reader how you want to describe the narrator's guilt. You might shape this question into a thesis by instead proposing an answer to that question: The narrator of "The Tell-Tale Heart" appears to be racked by guilt for the murder of his employer, but the tale leaves open the possibility that this guilt is merely feigned. Notice that this thesis provides an initial plan or structure for the rest of the paper; notice, too, that the thesis statement does not necessarily have to fit into one sentence. After raising the question of the narrator's guilt feelings, you could examine the related question of the narrator's putative madness. The thesis can raise the matter of guilt and use it to dig deeper into the narrator's character.

Moreover, remember that a good thesis makes an assertion that you need to support. In other words, a good thesis does not state the obvious. If you tried to formulate a thesis about the narrator by simply saying, The narrator of "The Tell-Tale Heart" is a man who murders his employer, you have done nothing but rephrase the obvious. The narrator says in the second paragraph that he has made up his mind to take the life of the old man, and he describes the killing in the 11th paragraph. Since this information is provided outright, there would be no point in spending three to five pages to support that assertion. You might try to develop a stronger thesis from an obvious one by asking yourself some further questions about your original point. Why does the narrator kill the old man? Why does he do so in such a peculiar manner? What feelings does the story elicit from us toward the narrator's crime? Such a line of questioning might lead you to a more viable thesis, like the one in the preceding paragraph.

As the comparison with the road map suggests, your thesis should appear near the beginning of the paper. In relatively short papers (three to six pages) the thesis almost always appears in the first paragraph. Some writers fall into the trap of saving the thesis for the end, trying to provide a surprise or a big moment of revelation, as if to say, "TA-DA! I've just proved that Poe uses the popularity of the insanity defense in the 1840s to show that his narrator is sane." Placing a thesis at the end of an essay can seriously mar the essay's effectiveness. If you fail to define your essay's point and purpose clearly at the beginning, your reader will find it difficult to assess your argument and understand the points you are making. If your argument comes as a surprise at the end, you force your reader to reread your essay in order to assess its logic and effectiveness.

Finally, you should avoid using the first person ("I") as you present your thesis. Though it is not strictly wrong to write in the first person, it is difficult to do so gracefully. While writing in the first person, beginning writers often fall into the trap of writing self-reflexive prose (writing *about* their paper *in* their paper). Often this leads to the most dreaded of opening lines: "In this paper I am going to discuss. . . ." Not only does this self-reflexive voice make for very awkward prose, it frequently allows writers to boldly announce a topic while completely avoiding a thesis statement. An example might be a paper that begins as follows: The Narrative of Arthur Gordon Pym, Poe's only novel, follows the adventures of Arthur Gordon Pym as he travels to the South Seas. In this paper, I am going to discuss the significance of the sea. The author of this paper has done no more than announce a topic for the paper (the significance of the sea). While the last sentence might be intended as a thesis, the writer fails to present an idea about the significance of the sea. To improve this "thesis," the writer would need to back up a couple of steps. First, the announced topic of the paper is too broad; literary scholars have discussed the symbolism of the sea for more than 100 years without yielding any one definitive interpretation. The writer should first consider some of the many functions of the sea within Poe's text. From here, one could select the function that seems most appealing and then begin to craft a specific thesis. A writer who chooses to explore the relationship between the sea and Pym's quest for identity, for example, could craft a thesis that reads, Pym's many travails on the ocean suggest that he experiences a symbolic rebirth.

Outlines

While developing a strong, thoughtful thesis early in your writing process should help focus your paper, outlining provides an essential tool for logically shaping that paper. A good outline helps you see—and develop—the relationships among the points in your argument and assures you that your paper flows logically and coherently. Outlining not only helps place your points in a logical order but also helps you subordinate supporting points, weed out irrelevant points, and decide if any necessary points are missing from your argument. Most of us are familiar with formal outlines that use numerical and letter designations for each point. However, there are different types of outlines; you may find that an informal outline is a more useful tool for you. What is important is that you spend the time to develop some sort of outline—formal or informal.

Remember that an outline is a tool to help you shape and write a strong paper. If you do not spend sufficient time planning your supporting points and shaping the arrangement of those points, you will most likely construct a vague, unfocused outline that provides little, if any, help with the writing of the paper. Consider the following example.

Thesis: The narrator of "The Tell-Tale Heart" has murdered the old man for his money, and he merely feigns madness to escape punishment.

   I. Introduction and thesis

  II. Narrator
     A. Nervousness
     B. Police arrival
     C. Ticking sounds
     D. Paranoia

 III. Evil eye

```
IV. Old man
    A. Interaction with old man

 V. Narrator is guilty

VI. Conclusion
    A. Narrator cannot use insanity defense
```

This outline has a number of flaws. First, the major topics labeled with the Roman numerals are not arranged in a logical order. If the paper's aim is to show how the narrator coveted the old man's money and then killed him, the writer should define those functions before presenting either the paranoia or the arrival of the police. Similarly, the thesis makes no mention of the evil eye, but the writer includes it as a major section of the outline. As a motive for murder, it may well have a place in the essay, but the writer fails to provide details about its place in the argument. Moreover, the writer includes "police arrival" as letter B under section II. Letters A, C, and D all refer to signs that indicate the narrator might be insane; the police arrival does not belong in this list. The writer could argue that it is, like the other three, an indication of the narrator's guilt, but unlike the other items it is not an indicator of insanity. Another problem is the inclusion of a letter A in sections IV and VI. An outline should not include an A without a B, a 1 without a 2, and so forth. The final problem with this outline, probably the most serious, is its overall lack of detail. None of the sections provides much information about the content of the argument, and it seems likely that the writer has not given sufficient thought to the content of the paper.

A better start to this outline might be the following:

```
Thesis: The narrator of "The Tell-Tale Heart" has murdered
the old man for his money, and he merely feigns madness
to escape punishment.

  I. Introduction and thesis

 II. Definition of legal insanity in 1843
```

III. Parallels between definition and narrator's behavior

IV. The ticking sounds as convincing evidence

V. The confession to the police as final evidence
   1. Their laughter
   2. His actions with chair

VI. Conclusion

This new outline would prove much more helpful when it came time to write the paper.

An outline like this could be shaped into an even more useful tool if the writer fleshed out the argument by providing specific examples from the text to support each point. Once you have listed your main point and your supporting ideas, develop this raw material by listing related supporting ideas and material under each of those main headings. From there, arrange the material in subsections and order the material logically.

For example, you might begin with one of the theses cited above: The narrator of "The Tell-Tale Heart" has murdered the old man for his money, and he merely feigns madness to escape punishment. As noted above, this thesis already gives you the beginning of an organization. Start by supporting the reasons on which you base your idea that the narrator is feigning insanity. You might begin your outline, then, with three topic headings: (1) narrator as possibly insane, (2) insanity defense in 1840s, and (3) narrator as faking insanity to cover up murder. Under each of those headings you could list ideas that support the particular point. Be sure to include references to parts of the text that help build your case.

An informal outline might look like this:

Thesis: The narrator of "The Tell-Tale Heart" has murdered the old man for his money, and he merely feigns madness to escape punishment.

1. Narrator's odd behavior
   - Narrator's fear of the evil eye
     - Superstitions about the evil eye were common
     - "I think it was his eye! yes, it was this!"
     - Superstitions about the evil eye can be found in a number of Poe tales, including "Metzengerstein" and "Ligeia." Note how the narrator refers to the eye as "pale blue" with a "film over it" and says that it is so fearful that his "blood ran cold"
   - Narrator's strange behavior with lantern
   - Narrator's hearing
     - He hears death watches in the wall
     - He hears the old man's "terror"
     - Narrator hears the old man's heart after his death; he calls it a "low dull, quick sound—much such a sound as a watch makes when enveloped in cotton"

2. Insanity defense
   - Contextually, "The Tell-Tale Heart" is a story of its time. Insanity defense was a popular topic in the news
   - Knowledge of a controversial new disease called "moral insanity" and of the legal and philosophical dilemmas that surrounded its discovery
   - Frame of reference for Poe's audience
     - Public suspicion of deception in such insanity pleas became widespread, and by 1840 trials featuring such defenses were major events, their proceedings splashed in detail across the front pages of the nation's daily newspapers

○ Before 1835, insanity plea rarely used. Changed in 1835 with awareness of moral insanity. Quickly became focus of extensive debate; filled thousands of pages of publications

○ Physicians of Poe's time regarded derangement of the faculty of hearing among the most common symptoms of insanity. Ticking and ringing sounds were singled out by Poe's contemporaries as common among the insane

3. Possibility that narrator is feigning insanity
   • Has been caught in the act of murder; needs an excuse
   • Poe's audience would start out with the possibility, if not the likelihood, that the narrator was feigning insanity
   • Poe's contemporaries would have made a connection from the ticking and ringing sounds to the suspect insanity defenses they knew so well
   • Possibility that murder is not due to insanity; motive could be money
     ○ Narrator mentions he had no "desire" for the old man's gold; shutters locked each night "through fear of robbers." Shows treasure to police
     ○ Poe's own financial woes are well known, and it was not unusual for his stories to contain references to money and murderers
   • Mad act at end could be faked: Police "mocked" his foams and raves

Conclusion:
   • The behavior of the police is most convincing in arguing against insanity. It is not

likely that they "chatted pleasantly, and smiled" in the face of a madman

- Solution not simple. The police deem narrator's madness feigned; story may be sardonic commentary on abuse of the insanity defense. Alternatively, story raises but leaves unsettled our doubt about narrator's madness

You would set about writing a formal outline in a similar way, though in the final stages you would label the headings differently. A formal outline for an essay on "The Masque of the Red Death" might look like the following:

Thesis: Poe uses masking and masquerade in "The Masque of the Red Death" to show how people attempt to hide from death.

I. Introduction and thesis

II. Poe's ideas about folly of using masquerade to avoid reality
   A. Prospero: character as artificer; he has created his own world
   B. Revelers pretending
      1. Drawn not as individuals but as a frenzied group
      2. Grotesque costumes
      3. Avoidance of the seventh room
      4. Behavior each time the clock ticks the hour

III. Colors of rooms
   A. Represent seven days of the week, seven deadly sins, or seven ages of man
   B. Black
      1. Final room in black and red
      2. The seventh apartment shrouded in black velvet tapestries

     3. Final room has a "gigantic clock of ebony"

     4. Associations with passage of time and death

     5. Metaphorical and literal meanings

  C. Red

     1. Particular uses in the story

     2. Death is personified as the Red Death

     3. Red is the color of blood

     4. Final chamber has window panes of red. "But in this chamber only, the color of the windows failed to correspond with the decorations. The panes here were scarlet—a deep blood color"

IV. Conclusion

  A. Stranger "shrouded from head to foot in the habiliments of the grave"

     1. His costume is "dabbled in blood"

     2. Red Death represents both a literal and figurative death

  B. How Prospero uses occasion of masquerade fruitlessly to try to avoid death

     1. rushes from the blue room to the seventh black room

     2. Prospero confronted by the masked death

     3. Red Death represents death; retreat of Prospero and guests to secluded abbey seen as attempt of human beings to deny inevitability of their own mortality

As in the previous example, the thesis provides the seeds of a structure, and the writer is careful to arrange the supporting points in a logical manner, showing the relationships among the ideas in the paper.

Body Paragraphs

Once your outline is complete, you can begin drafting your paper. Paragraphs, units of related sentences, are the building blocks of a good paper, and as you draft you should keep in mind both the function and the qualities of good paragraphs. Paragraphs help you chart and control the shape and content of your essay, and they help the reader see your organization and your logic. You should begin a new paragraph whenever you move from one major point to another. In longer, more complex essays you might use a group of related paragraphs to support major points. Remember that in addition to being adequately developed, a good paragraph is both unified and coherent.

Unified Paragraphs

Each paragraph must be centralized around one idea or point, and a unified paragraph carefully focuses on and develops this central idea without including extraneous ideas or tangents. For beginning writers, the best way to ensure that you are constructing unified paragraphs is to include a topic sentence in each paragraph. This topic sentence should convey the main point of the paragraph, and every sentence in the paragraph should relate to that topic sentence. Any sentence that strays from the central topic does not belong in the paragraph and needs to be revised or deleted. Consider the following paragraph about how the narrator of "The Tell-Tale Heart" proves himself insane through his irrational logic. Notice how the paragraph veers away from the main point that the narrator's logic proves his insanity:

> The narrator of "The Tell-Tale Heart" would have the reader believe that he is sane because he is logical; the methodical behavior he describes, however, does not seem sane, but insane. The story's opening paragraph introduces the conflict that drives the story's plot. The narrator asks a key question: "why will you say that I am mad?" He then suggests that his calm logic demonstrates his sanity. The remainder of the story is the narrator's account of how he rationally behaved in killing the old man. The narrator says that he killed the old man just because he did not like the way his

eye, which "resembled that of a vulture," caused him to be uncomfortable (792). It does not take long for the reader to see that the narrator is crazy. He talks incessantly about the old man and his eye. Even the narrator's word choice in the second paragraph hints that the narrator is obsessed with the eye: "I think it was his eye!" he exclaims. "[Y]es it was this" (792).

Although the paragraph begins solidly and the first sentence provides the central theme, the author soon goes on a tangent. If the purpose of the paragraph is to demonstrate that the narrator's logical behavior shows his madness, the sentences about the old man's eye do not support that idea. Mention of the eye may find a place later in the paper, but it should be deleted from this paragraph.

Coherent Paragraphs

In addition to shaping unified paragraphs, you must also craft coherent paragraphs, paragraphs that develop their points logically with sentences that flow smoothly into one another. Coherence depends on the order of your sentences, but it is not strictly the order of the sentences that is important to paragraph coherence. You also need to craft your prose to help the reader see the relationship among the sentences.

Consider the following paragraph about the narrator's attempts to feign madness in "The Tell-Tale Heart." Notice how the writer uses the same ideas as the paragraph above yet fails to help the reader see the relationships among the points:

The narrator of "The Tell-Tale Heart" would have the reader believe that he is sane. The methodical behavior he describes does not seem sane, but insane. The story's opening paragraph introduces the conflict that drives the story's plot. The narrator asks a key question: "Why *will* you say that I am mad?" The remainder of the story is the narrator's account of how he rationally behaved in killing the old man. The narrator says that he killed the old man just because he did not like the way his eye, which "resembled that of a vulture," caused him to be uncomfortable (792). The reader soon sees that the narrator is crazy. He talks incessantly about the old man and his eye. The narrator's word choice in the second paragraph hints that the narrator is obsessed with the eye. He exclaims, "I think it was his eye! yes it was this!" (792).

This paragraph demonstrates that unity alone does not guarantee paragraph effectiveness. The argument is hard to follow because the author fails both to show connections between the sentences and to indicate how they work to support the overall point.

A number of techniques are available to aid paragraph coherence. Careful use of transitional words and phrases is essential. You can use transitional flags to introduce an example or an illustration (*for example, for instance*), to amplify a point or add another phase of the same idea (*additionally, furthermore, next, similarly, finally, then*), to indicate a conclusion or result (*therefore, as a result, thus, in other words*), to signal a contrast or a qualification (*on the other hand, nevertheless, despite this, on the contrary, still, however, conversely*), to signal a comparison (*likewise, in comparison, similarly*), and to indicate a movement in time (*afterward, earlier, eventually, finally, later, subsequently, until*).

In addition to transitional flags, careful use of pronouns aids coherence and flow. If you were writing about *The Wizard of Oz,* you would not want to keep repeating the phrase *the witch* or the name *Dorothy.* Careful substitution of the pronoun *she* in these instances can aid coherence. A word of warning, though: When you substitute pronouns for proper names, always be sure that your pronoun reference is clear. In a paragraph that discusses both Dorothy and the witch, substituting *she* could lead to confusion. Make sure that it is clear to whom the pronoun refers. Generally, the pronoun refers to the last person you have referred to.

While repeating the same name over and over again can lead to awkward, boring prose, it is possible to use repetition to help your paragraph's coherence. Careful repetition of important words or phrases can lend coherence to your paragraph by reminding readers of your key points. Admittedly, it takes some practice to use this technique effectively. Reading your prose aloud can help you develop an ear for effective use of repetition.

To see how helpful transitional aids are, compare the paragraph below to the preceding paragraph about the narrator's insanity. Notice how the author works with the same ideas and quotations but shapes them into a much more coherent paragraph whose point is clearer and easier to follow:

> The narrator of "The Tell-Tale Heart" would have the reader believe that he is sane because he is logical; the methodical behavior he describes, however, does not seem sane, but insane. The story's opening paragraph introduces the conflict that drives the story's plot. The narrator asks a key question: "Why *will* you say that I am mad?" (792). He then suggests that his calm logic demonstrates his sanity. The remainder of the story is the narrator's account of how he rationally behaved in killing the old man. The narrator says that he killed the old man just because he did not like the way his eye, which "resembled that of a vulture," caused him to be uncomfortable (792). It does not take long for the reader to see that the narrator is crazy. He talks incessantly about the old man and his eye. Even the narrator's word choice in the second paragraph hints that the narrator is obsessed with the eye. "I think it was his eye!" he exclaims. "[Y]es it was this" (792). A reader may wonder why, if the police were satisfied, they decided to stick around and chat at five o'clock in the morning. Most likely their strategy was to wait for him to crack, and indeed their presence, which the narrator acknowledges makes him uncomfortable, has precisely this effect. He begins hearing things; his manner becomes agitated and then violent. He foams, he raves, he swears; he swings his chair. The narrator speaks of the policemen's "derision" and "hypocritical smiles" (797). Many readers assume that the narrator only imagines these reactions because his behavior indicates insanity.

Similarly, the following paragraph from a paper on the use of the gothic in "Ligeia" demonstrates both unity and coherence. In it, the author argues that Poe uses traditional gothic elements in ironic ways to bend the genre into a new form.

> Interpretation of "Ligeia" stumbles awkwardly among the rocks of its seemingly disparate elements: its irony and its horror, its unbelievability, and its overwrought earnestness. Each of these elements has been observed and widely discussed. Debate has centered, however, on which of these elements is really at work in the story, or at least which is primary, when a truly satisfactory reading should account for them all. Such a reading comes together when we recognize the nature of the narrator's duplicity. This man is a gothicist, who lives in a remote, decaying abbey, furnished in a gaudy "semi-gothic" style. His wife lies dead, poisoned. He says he did not do it: He thinks perhaps his former wife, come back from the dead, did it, but he cannot be sure, poor soul, because he is an opium addict and not in control of his faculties. "Ligeia," then, is this man's cover story. Immersed in gothics as he is, he tells a tale that is itself a gothic, cobbled together with familiar plot elements, conventional devices, and sensational prose. Viewed in this light, his story appears ludicrous, but at the same time, his tale unintentionally reveals a truly shocking sequence of events. The interplay of the true horrors and the ridiculous cover story thus create a new work: a sort of hypergothic that travesties the genre and at the same time wallows in it.

Introductions

Introductions present particular challenges for writers. Generally, your introduction should do two things: capture your reader's attention and explain the main point of your essay. In other words, while your introduction should contain your thesis, it needs to do a bit more work than that. You are likely to find that starting that first paragraph is one of the most difficult parts of the paper. It is hard to face that blank page or screen, and as a result, many beginning writers, in desperation to start somewhere, begin with overly broad, general statements. While it is often a good strategy to start with more general subject matter and narrow your focus, do not begin with broad sweeping statements such as, A defini-tion of insanity would be killing someone, or Throughout the history of literature, many authors have used insane narrators to prove their points. Such sentences are nothing but empty filler. They begin to fill the blank page, but they do nothing to advance your argument. Instead, you might try to gain your readers' inter-est. Some writers like to begin with a pertinent quotation or a relevant question. Or you might begin with an introduction of the topic you will discuss. If you are writing about Poe's use of the insanity defense in "The Tell-Tale Heart," for instance, you might begin by talking about the history of the insanity defense. Another mistake to avoid is depending on your title to introduce the author and the text you are writing about. Always include the work's author and title in your opening paragraph.

Compare the effectiveness of the following introductions:

1. Things are not always as they appear. It is at least possible and perhaps likely that the narrator murdered the old man for his money and has merely feigned madness to escape punishment. Such a reading finds strong support in the text.

2. Edgar Allan Poe's "The Tell-Tale Heart" begins with a question: "Why *will* you say that I am mad?" Despite the denial this question implies, most modern readers do not hesitate to pronounce the man mad. There is, however, much room for doubt. It is at least possible and perhaps likely that the narrator murdered the old man for his money and has merely feigned madness to escape punishment. Such a reading finds strong support in the text. The historical context of the tale also supports such a reading, for at the time the story appeared, in January 1843, the issue of insanity as a defense against a charge of murder was one of the most prominent public issues.

The first introduction begins with a boring, overly broad sentence and then moves abruptly to the thesis. Notice, too, how a reader deprived of the paper's title does not know the title of the story that the paper will analyze. The second introduction works with the same material and thesis but provides more detail and is consequently much more interesting. It begins by discussing the possibility that the narrator may not be mad, as many suspect, and then speaks briefly about textual and historical support for the thesis. Note that the paragraph includes the thesis as well as the author and the title of the work to be discussed.

The paragraph below provides an example of a different opening. It begins by introducing the author and the text it will analyze and then briefly introduces relevant details in order to set up its thesis:

> The narrator of Edgar Allan Poe's "The Black Cat" actually tells us he is lying in his first breath. "For the most wild yet most homely narrative which I am about to pen," he begins, "I neither expect nor solicit belief. Mad indeed would I be to expect it, in a case where my very senses reject their own evidence. Yet, mad am I not—and very surely do I not dream" (840). If the man is neither mad nor mistaken and yet is not to be believed, it can only be that he is lying. Such open admission of unreliability, prevalent among Poe's narrators, is also characteristic of real-life liars. It is also a literary signal: an announcement that the game is afoot. In effect, the narrator defies the reader to find him out, just as he recklessly defies the police by calling attention to the wall that conceals his wife's body. Recognizing that the narrator is lying gives us the vantage point from which we are able to discover the hidden truth. What we will discover seems at first astonishing: that the narrator murdered his wife not impulsively on the cellar stairs, as he asserts, but willfully and with malice aforethought at the time he claims to have killed his cat.

Conclusions

Conclusions present another series of challenges for writers. No doubt you have heard the old adage about writing papers: "Tell us what you are going to say, say it, and then tell us what you've said." While this formula does not necessarily result in bad papers, it does not necessarily result in good ones, either. It will almost certainly result in boring papers (especially boring conclusions). If you have done a good job establishing your points in the body of the paper, the reader already knows and understands your argument. There is no need to merely reiterate. Do not just summarize your main points in your conclusion. Such a dull and mechanical conclusion does nothing to advance your argument or interest your reader. Consider the following conclusion to the paper about the insanity defense in "The Tell-Tale Heart."

> In conclusion, Poe uses the insanity defense of the 1840s to tell his reader about a possibly insane narrator. The narrator's behavior seems crazy, and so does his manner of telling it. But other evidence, especially the reaction of the policemen, suggests that he may be feigning insanity. In the end, either interpretation is possible.

Besides starting with a mechanical and obvious transitional device, this conclusion does little more than summarize the main points of the outline (and it does not even touch on all of them). It is incomplete and uninteresting.

Instead, your conclusion should add something to your paper. A good tactic is to build upon the points you have been arguing. Asking *why?* often helps you draw further conclusions. For example, in the paper on "The Tell-Tale Heart," you might speculate or explain why the tale leaves us uncertain whether the narrator is mad. Another method of successfully concluding a paper is to speculate on other directions in which to take your topic by tying it into larger issues. You might do this by envisioning your paper as just one section of a larger paper. Having established your points in this paper, how would you build upon this argument? Where would you go next? In the following conclusion to a paper on "The Tell-Tale Heart," the author reiterates some of the main points of the paper but does so in order to amplify the discussion of the story's bending of genres.

> We end up with a picture of a man as clever as he claims to be. Yet the portrait is by no means a simple one. We may deem the policemen's reaction as decisive, conclude that the narrator's madness is feigned, and read the story as

a sardonic commentary on the prevailing widespread abuse of the insanity defense. Alternatively, we may conclude that the story raises but leaves unsettled our doubt that the narrator is mad. (Unlike "The Black Cat," which tells us that the narrator's story has failed to save him from execution, "The Tell-Tale Heart" does not reveal whether the narrator's defense is successful.) A reading in which the question of sanity remains unresolved tends to draw us into philosophical reflection upon what constitutes sanity, or whether a man who can calmly plan and execute a brutal murder has not in a sense taken more complete leave of his senses than a man who acts from passion or obvious derangement. We find ourselves confronting an intriguing puzzle indeed: a tale that is both detective story and tale of terror, hinting at satire upon a topical debate while inviting earnest reflection on the wider issues of sanity. It is a text situated, like other Poe stories, at a frontier where genres bend and merge.

Citations and Formatting

Using Primary Sources

As the examples included in this chapter indicate, strong papers on literary texts incorporate quotations from the text in order to support their points. It is not enough for you to assert your interpretation; you must also provide support with evidence from the text. Without well-chosen quotations to support your argument, you are, in effect, saying to the reader, "Take my word for it." It is important to use quotations thoughtfully and selectively. Remember that the paper presents *your* argument, so choose quotations that support *your* assertions. Do not let the author's voice overwhelm your own. With that caution in mind, there are some guidelines you should follow to ensure that you use quotations clearly and effectively.

Integrating Quotations:

Quotations should always be integrated into your own prose. Do not just drop them into your paper without introduction or comment. Otherwise, it is unlikely that your reader will see their function. You can integrate textual support easily and clearly with identifying tags, short phrases that identify the speaker. For example:

```
The narrator says of Ligeia that in "beauty of face no
maiden ever equaled her" (311).
```

While this tag appears before the quotation, you can also use tags after or in the middle of the quoted text, as the following examples demonstrate:

```
"Ligeia had brought me far more, very far more than
ordinarily falls to the lot of mortals," claims the
narrator (320).
```

```
"What inexpressible madness seized me with that thought?"
the narrator says after Lady Rowena dies. "One bound,
and I had reached her feet!" (330).
```

You can also use a colon to formally introduce a quotation:

```
The narrator's awe is clear: "I have spoken of the
learning of Ligeia: it was immense—such as I have never
known in woman" (315).
```

When you quote brief sections of poems (three lines or fewer), use a slash mark with a space on each side to indicate the line breaks in the poem:

```
As the poem ends, Ligeia speaks of the power of death:
the "play is the tragedy, 'Man,' / And its hero the
Conqueror Worm."
```

Longer quotations (more than four lines of prose or three lines of poetry) should be set off from the rest of your paper in a block quotation. Double-space before you begin the passage, indent 10 spaces from your left-hand margin, and double-space the passage itself. Because the indentation signals the inclusion of a quotation, do not use quotation marks around the cited passage. Use a colon to introduce the passage:

```
The narrator speaks lovingly of Ligeia:

    In stature she was tall, somewhat slender, and in
    her latter days, even emaciated. I would in vain
```

> attempt to portray the majesty, the quiet ease, of her demeanor, or the incomprehensible lightness and elasticity of her footfall. She came and departed as a shadow. I was never made aware of her low sweet voice, as she placed her marble hand upon my shoulder. In beauty of face no maiden ever equaled her. (311)

The whole of Ligeia's poem speaks of fear:

> But see, amid the mimic rout,
>   A crawling shape intrude!
> A blood-red thing that writhes from out
>   The scenic solitude!
> It writhes!—it writhes!—with mortal pangs
>   The mimes become its food,
> And the seraphs sob at vermin fangs
>   In human gore imbued. (319)

Clearly, Ligeia witnesses a scene of violence.

It is also important to interpret quotations after you introduce them and explain how they help advance your point. The preceding excerpt does so with a single sentence, but often you will wish to explain more fully. You cannot assume that your reader will interpret the quotations the same way that you do.

Quote Accurately:

Take pains to quote precisely. Anything within quotations marks must be the author's exact words. There are some rules to follow if you need to modify the quotation to fit into your prose.

1. Use brackets to indicate any material that has been added to the author's exact wording. For example, if you need to add any words to the quotation or alter it grammatically to allow it to fit into your prose, indicate your changes in brackets:

> After Ligeia dies, the narrator marries again,
> and his second wife is afraid of the bedroom
> they share. "One night, near the closing in of
> September, [Lady Rowena] pressed this distressing
> subject with more than usual emphasis upon my
> attention" (324).

2. Conversely, if you choose to omit any words from the quotation, use ellipses (three spaced periods) to indicate missing words or phrases:

> The narrator is enamored of Ligeia's beauty,
> saying that in "stature she was tall, somewhat
> slender . . . even emaciated" (310).

3. If you delete a sentence or more, use the ellipses after a period:

> The narrator speaks of Ligeia's beauty, saying
> that in "stature she was tall. . . . In beauty
> of face no maiden ever equaled her" (310).

4. If you omit a line or more of poetry, or more than one paragraph of prose, use a single line of spaced periods to indicate the omission:

> But see, amid the mimic rout,
> A crawling shape intrude!
> . . . .
> It writhes!—it writhes!—with mortal pangs
> The mimes become its food,
> And the seraphs sob at vermin fangs
> In human gore imbued. (319)

Punctuate Properly:
Punctuation of quotations often causes more trouble than it should. Once again, you just need to keep these simple rules in mind.

1. Periods and commas should be placed inside quotation marks, even if they are not part of the original quotation:

> The narrator says of Ligeia that her "radiance" was like that of "an opium dream."

The only exception to this rule is when the quotation is followed by a parenthetical reference. In this case, the period or comma goes after the citation (more on these later in this chapter):

> The narrator says of Ligeia that in "beauty of face no maiden ever equaled her" (311).

2. Other marks of punctuation—colons, semicolons, question marks, and exclamation points—go outside the quotation marks unless they are part of the original quotation:

> Why does the narrator refer to the early days of his marriage to Lady Rowena as "unhallowed hours"?

> The narrator of "The Tell-Tale Heart" asks, "Why will you say that I am mad?"

Documenting Primary Sources

Unless you are instructed otherwise, you should provide sufficient information for your reader to locate material you quote. Generally, literature papers follow the rules set forth by the Modern Language Association (MLA). These can be found in the *MLA Handbook for Writers of Research Papers* (sixth edition). You should be able to find this book in the reference section of your library. Additionally, its rules for citing both primary and secondary sources are widely available from online sources. One of these is the Online Writing Lab [OWL] at Purdue University. OWL's guide to MLA style is available at http://owl.english.purdue.edu/owl/resource/557/01/. The Modern Language Association also offers answers to frequently asked questions about MLA style on this helpful Web page: http://www.mla.org/style_faq. Generally, when you cite from literary works in papers, you should keep a few guidelines in mind.

Parenthetical Citations:

MLA asks for parenthetical references in your text after quotations. When you are working with prose (short stories, novels, or essays), include page numbers in the parentheses:

> The narrator says of Ligeia that in "beauty of face no maiden ever equaled her" (311).

When you are quoting poetry, include line numbers:

> Ligeia speaks of evil things: "But see, amid the mimic rout, / A crawling shape intrude!" (25-26)

Works Cited Page:

Parenthetical citations are linked to a separate Works Cited page at the end of the paper. The Works Cited page lists works alphabetically by the authors' last name. An entry for the above reference to Poe's "Ligeia" would read:

> Poe, Edgar Allan. "Ligeia." *Collected Works of Edgar Allan Poe*. Ed. Thomas Ollive Mabbott. Cambridge: Harvard UP, 1978. 305–334.

The *MLA Handbook* includes a full listing of sample entries, as do many of the online explanations of MLA style.

Documenting Secondary Sources

To ensure that your paper is built entirely upon your own ideas and analysis, instructors often ask that you write interpretative papers without any outside research. If, on the other hand, your paper requires research, you must document any secondary sources you use. You need to document direct quotations, summaries or paraphrases of others' ideas, and factual information that is not common knowledge. Follow the guidelines above for quoting primary sources when you use direct quotations from secondary sources. Keep in mind that MLA style also includes specific guidelines for citing electronic sources. OWL's Web site provides a good summary: http://owl.english.purdue.edu/owl/resource/557/09/.

Parenthetical Citations:

As with the documentation of primary sources, described above, MLA guidelines require in-text parenthetical references to your secondary sources. Unlike the research papers you might write for a history class, literary research papers following MLA style do not use footnotes as a means of documenting sources. Instead, after a quotation, you should cite the author's last name and the page number:

> Before 1835, insanity pleas had been entered only in the defense of idiots or raving maniacs, for according to a contemporary work on jurisprudence, only someone "totally deprived of his understanding" and no more aware of what he was doing "than an infant . . . a brute, or a wild beast" could be judged legally insane (Haslam 31).

If you include the name of the author in your prose, then you would include only the page number in your citation. For example:

> According to John Haslam, only someone "totally deprived of his understanding" and no more aware of what he was doing "than an infant . . . a brute, or a wild beast" could be judged legally insane (31).

If your essay cites more than one work by the same author, the parenthetical citation should include a shortened yet identifiable version of the title to indicate which of the author's works you are currently citing from. For example:

> According to John Halsam, insanity as a legal defense only began in the 19th century (*Illustrations* 27).

If you summarize or paraphrase the particular ideas of your source, even if you do not use exact quotes, you must provide similar documentation:

> Some readers might believe that the narrator is feigning madness. Public suspicion of deception in such insanity

pleas became widespread, and by 1840 trials featuring
such defenses were major events, their proceedings
splashed in detail across the front pages of the nation's
daily newspapers (Bynum 144).

Works Cited Page:

Like the primary sources discussed above, the parenthetical references to
secondary sources are keyed to a separate works cited page at the end of
the paper. Here is an excerpt of a works cited page that uses the examples
cited above. Note that when two or more works by the same author are
listed, you should use three hyphens followed by a period in the subsequent entries. You can find a complete list of sample entries in the *MLA
Handbook* or from an online summary of MLA style.

WORKS CITED

Bynum, Paige-Matthey. " 'Observe How Healthily—How Calmly
I Tell You the Whole Story': Moral Insanity and
Edgar Allan Poe's 'The Tell-Tale Heart.' " *Literature
and Science as Modes of Expression*. Ed. Frederick
Amrine. Boston: Kluwer, 1989. 141–52.

Haslam, John. "The Nature of Madness." *Madness and Morals:
Ideas on Insanity in the Nineteenth Century*. Ed. V.
Skultans. Boston: Routledge and Kegan Paul, 1975.

——. *Illustrations of Madness*. New York: Arno Press,
1976. 31.

Plagiarism

Failure to document your sources carefully and thoroughly can leave
you open to charges of stealing the ideas of others, which is known as
plagiarism and is a very serious matter. Remember that it is important to
use quotation marks when you use language used by your source, even
if you use just one or two words. For example, if you wrote, someone
totally deprived of his understanding and no more
aware of what he was doing than an infant, a brute, or
a wild beast could be judged legally insane, you would be
guilty of plagiarism, since you used Haslam's distinct language without
acknowledging him as the source. Instead, you should write: to be
judged insane a person had to be "totally deprived of

his understanding" and no more aware of what he was doing "than an infant . . . a brute, or a wild beast" (Haslam 31). In this case, you have properly credited Haslam.

Neither summarizing the ideas of an author nor changing or omitting some words allows you to omit a citation. Kenneth Silverman's biography of Poe contains the following passage about Poe's writing style:

> With his proclaimed ability to write in a variety of styles, Poe prided himself on his humor, although it rarely found subtler expression than heavy-handed parody, slapstick with a brutal edge, and phunny phellow wordplay featuring flatulent names like Flatzplatz. He more convincingly remarked of himself that he was "not 'of the merry mood'" (Silverman 204).

Below are two examples of plagiarized passages:

> Poe was proud of his humor, although it was not subtle; he used humor with a cutting edge, funny wordplay, and silly names.

> Poe often used unsubtle slapstick with a brutal edge, featuring silly names, but he admitted that he was not of the merry mood (Silverman 204).

While the first passage doesn't use Silverman's exact language, it does have the same ideas. Since these ideas are distinctly Silverman's, the excerpt constitutes plagiarism. The second passage has shortened his passage, changed some wording, and included a citation, but some of the phrasing is Silverman's. The first passage could be fixed simply by adding a parenthetical citation. The second passage would require the use of quotation marks in addition to the parenthetical citation. The passage below represents an honestly and adequately documented use of the original passage:

> According to Kenneth Silverman, Poe's humor was often "slapstick with a brutal edge and phunny phellow wordplay featuring flatulent names like Flatzplatz" (204).

This passage acknowledges that the phrasing is Silverman's and appropriately uses quotation marks to indicate his exact words.

While it is not necessary to document well-known facts, often referred to as "common knowledge," any ideas or language that you take from someone else must be properly documented. Common knowledge generally includes the birth and death dates of authors or other well-documented facts of their lives. An often-cited guideline is that if you can find the information in three sources, it is common knowledge. Despite this guideline, it is, admittedly, often difficult to know if the facts you uncover are common knowledge or not. When in doubt, document your source.

Sample Essay

Brigid O'Shaughnessy
Professor M. Archer
English 310
May 23, 2007

THE INSANITY DEFENSE AND "THE TELL-TALE HEART"

"The Tell-Tale Heart" begins with a question: "Why *will* you say that I am mad?" Yet this question, and the denial it implies, has given modern readers little pause. But there is much room for doubt. It is possible and perhaps likely that the narrator murdered the old man for his money and has merely feigned madness to escape punishment. Such a reading finds strong support in the text. The historical context of the tale also supports such a reading, for at the time the story appeared, in January 1843, the issue of insanity as a defense against a charge of murder was one of the most prominent public issues.

Before 1835, insanity pleas had been entered only in the defense of idiots and raving maniacs, for, according to a contemporary work on jurisprudence, only someone "totally deprived of his understanding" and no more aware of what he was doing "than an infant . . . a brute, or a wild beast" could be judged legally insane (Haslam 31). The situation changed beginning in 1835 with the publication of a book by James Cowles Prichard that popularized the notion of "moral insanity," a condition in which a person, while retaining his intellectual faculties, is nevertheless considered incapable of "conducting himself with decency or propriety" (4–5).

Soon defenses on the grounds of moral insanity began leading to acquittals of violent criminals who seemed in perfect possession of their senses. Public suspicion of deception in such pleas became widespread, and by 1840 trials featuring such defenses were major events, their proceedings splashed in detail across the front pages of the nation's daily newspapers (Bynum 144).

Several features of the insanity trials of the day have relevance for the story. One is the narrator's hypersensitivity to noise. To the uninitiated, the noises the narrator claims to hear may well suggest madness, but to the skeptic of Poe's time they would have been so familiar as to seem pat. Physicians of the time regarded derangement of the faculty of hearing among the most common symptoms of insanity (Bynum 147). Defendants' claims of hearing ticking and ringing sounds in particular, and specific references to the noises of clocks appeared frequently in trial reports of the 1830s and 1840s (147). Poe's contemporaries, therefore, unlike modern readers, who focus on the horror the sounds inspire, might have been expected to make an immediate connection from these sounds to the suspect insanity defenses they knew so well.

A similar point may be made about the narrator's supposed obsession with the old man's eye. Taking at face value the claim that this was what motivated the murderer, critics have advanced a wide range of theories as to what the eye might represent. Suggestions include parental authority (Frank); the "evil eye" of tradition, believed capable of inflicting injury on those at whom it is directed (Kirkland); and an emblem of mortality or of subjection to time (Hoffman, Ketterer). But we should bear in mind that in Poe's time the evil eye was a commonplace, and the notion that the insane were afraid to look into people's eyes was popular belief (Bynum 146).

A third feature is the issue of concealing or revealing the crime. This matter was central to insanity pleas in Poe's time because it provided evidence of the defendant's knowledge of wrongdoing. Attempts at concealment were regarded as compelling evidence that the defendant was sane, while confessions constituted equally compelling evidence of insanity. Poe's tale contains both: the narrator's careful dismemberment of the old man's body and concealment of it under the floorboards and his subsequent revelation at the end of the tale.

Poe's manifest interest—and that of his readers—in feigned insanity invites us to view "The Tell-Tale Heart" not as a study of madness but of authorial deceit. Traditional readings start with the narrator's insanity as a given and go in search of the meaning of his madness. If instead we read his words as one would read the account of a murderer fairly caught in the act, the conclusion we would most likely draw is that the narrator killed the old man for his money; that when the police came, he told them the man was away, but when it became clear that his story was not working, he put on a "mad" act, which led to his revealing the body; and that he then concocted, after the fact, a tale to fit the madness plea, reaching for what were then the most familiar signs of madness.

To construct a sequence of events and decide what is true and what is a lie, a reader should rely on guidelines based on common experience. One of the first is that we give the greatest credence to statements that can be corroborated by others. Let us start, then, at the end of the story, when the policemen are present. We take it that the narrator's account is here at its most accurate, and what he says is that he acts mad in front of the policemen, and they laugh at his mad act. This he says very plainly, yet such is the text's construction—and the stance of the reader—that we simply do not take him at his word.

After he has shown the policemen around the house, the narrator claims, the men are satisfied. But his professed confidence seems doubtful. Police officers dispatched on "suspicion of foul play" (796) are not easily convinced by a suspect's seemingly carefree manner. Most likely their strategy was to string their suspect along, waiting for him to crack, and indeed their presence, which the narrator acknowledges makes him uncomfortable, has precisely this effect. He begins hearing things, he says; his manner becomes agitated, then violent. He foams; he raves; he swears; he swings his chair. What is the policemen's reaction now? The narrator speaks of their "derision" and "hypocritical smiles" (797). The police are smiling. But why? A suspected murderer becomes violent, and policemen smile? Surely they would not smile at a violent man they believed genuinely insane. The narrator tells us, "[T]hey were making a mockery of my horror!" (797). What else can this mean but that they did not believe his mad act? Furthermore, after saying that the policemen "suspected!—they knew!" and were mocking his horror, the narrator adds, "This I thought, and this I think" (797), a comment that casts the assertion not as one of many fleeting impressions but as a settled conviction that remains firm even in retrospect.

Also noteworthy is the odd wording the narrator employs in describing his growing agitation, his professed hallucinations. He says, "I fancied a ringing in my ears" (797), a statement that is neither logical nor idiomatic. We typically say either that we "imagined that we *heard* something" or that we "*heard* something

in our ears." To *"imagine* a ringing *in one's ears"* is
a redundancy that taken literally would suggest that
one is pretending to be hearing things. The word *fancy*
only strengthens such a reading. More important, his
final sentences state outright that it was not the
fancied ringing that drove the narrator to reveal the
body. Although he does refer to the ringing and the
beating of the dead man's heart, these—the effects of
his supposed madness—are not what motivate him; it is
the disbelief of the police:

> Anything was more tolerable than this derision!
> I could bear their hypocritical smiles no longer!
> I felt that I must scream or die!—and now—again!—
> hark! louder! louder! louder! *louder!*
>
> "Villains!" I shrieked, "dissemble no more! I
> admit the deed!—tear up the planks!—here, here!—it
> is the beating of his hideous heart! (797)

When his mad act does not work, he is forced to play
his trump card, revealing his crime.

How, then, shall the rest of his story be interpreted?
The young man must now make shift as best he can to
concoct a story that will support his feigned insanity.
In the rest of his narrative he can take greater
liberties with the truth, since there is no one to
contradict him. We should expect him to lie, and we
should be alert for elements in his story that suggest
mendacity. One has only to look for such lapses, and
they become prominent.

Consider his claim that the murder was motiveless.
The skeptical reader will feel no obligation whatsoever
to accept this claim, even stated as flatly as it
appears to be in the simple declarative, "Object there
was none" (792). A defendant in a murder trial would be
counted on to make his pretense of insanity credible in

the only way possible: by professing to have had either no reason at all for killing the man or a nutty one. The narrator begins by claiming the former ("Object there was none") and then goes on to claim the latter ("I think it was his eye! yes, it was this!").

Moreover, examination of the crucial passage reveals the most suspicious language in the story: "Object there was none. Passion there was none. I loved the old man. He had never wronged me. He had never given me insult. For his gold I had no desire. I think it was his eye! yes, it was this!" (792). He thinks it was the man's eye? The narrator would have us believe that he was so obsessed with the old man's eye that it drove him to murder, and then only when he had spent eight nights attempting to shine a light onto it, and now he says he thinks it was the eye. And more than that, the line "Yes, it was this" clearly indicates that the narrator has only now—as he is telling the story—hit upon this motive. Again, it is absurd to think that he obsessed over the eye for so long and only now realizes the fact. But if we read the story, as suggested in this essay, as the testimony of a man caught with a dead body to account for, then his phrasing makes perfect sense. To establish a plea of insanity, he must declare that his action was not rationally motivated. He begins with simple denial, listing and dismissing common motives for murder, delaying until the end the obvious motive of money. From here he shifts, at first tentatively and then positively, to an alternative explanation. The phrasing "For his gold I had no desire. I think it was his eye! yes, it was this!" captures the process of his working out his story.

Having taken the position that the narrator's insanity might be feigned, a reader seeks a rational motive for the crime. One supposition is money. The odd phrasing of the narrator's denial reinforces that suspicion and leads the reader to posit the substitution of eye for money. We should now examine the ensuing text for further evidence of the money motive, and specifically, we should apply the substitution of eye for money to see whether it proves helpful in structuring the text.

Such an approach leads us directly to the part of the story in which the narrator describes his nightly search with the lantern. Taken as presented, this is certainly the maddest behavior in the tale. We understand that he is trying to make us believe him mad and that part of his strategy is to claim to be sane. This strategy is far from deep: Almost anyone in his position would hit upon it as more effective than insensible raving. So when he says, "You should have seen how wisely I proceeded" (792) and then describes behavior of utter lunacy, we realize his method. We conclude that he did not really act in the insane way he describes, but at the same time we believe that his description does contain some kernel of truth. This we believe on two grounds. The first is experiential: We know that liars in real life more often alter facts than invent them. The second is literary: It is axiomatic that a mystery must provide means for its solution or, more generally, that texts must provide the means for their construction. The narrator's statements should therefore refer to something, which it should be possible for us to guess.

We take it, then, that something was happening all those nights, but not the pointless and unbelievable shining of the lantern. Applying the substitution of "gold" for "eye" provides the answer at once: The narrator was searching for the old man's gold. His statement that he "found the eye always closed; and so it was impossible to do the work" (793) translates into the man's money being hidden or locked up. The narrator could not carry out the murder until he had secured the treasure. (Doing so was evidently no simple matter, since it took eight nights of trying; it therefore could not have been safely postponed until after the murder.) We know that the old man kept money in his house because we are told that the shutters were locked, through fear of robbers (793), and we learn that the narrator found the old man's stash when he shows it to the police. Their interest in the man's money serves to reinforce our own.

We find ourselves confronting an intriguing puzzle indeed: a tale that is both detective story and tale of terror, hinting at satire upon a topical debate while inviting earnest reflection on the wider issues of sanity. The text is situated, like other Poe stories, at a frontier where genres bend and merge.

WORKS CITED

Bynum, Paige-Matthey. " 'Observe How Healthily—How Calmly I Tell You the Whole Story': Moral Insanity and Edgar Allan Poe's 'The Tell-Tale Heart.' " *Literature and Science as Modes of Expression.* Ed. Frederick Amrine. Boston: Kluwer, 1989. 141–52.

Frank, F. S. "Neighborhood Gothic: Poe's 'The Tell-Tale Heart.' " *The Sphinx: A Magazine of Literature and Society* 3 (1981): 53–60.

Haslam, J. "The Nature of Madness." *Madness and Morals: Ideas on Insanity in the Nineteenth Century.* Ed. V. Skultans. Boston: Routledge and Kegan Paul, 1975. 31.

Hoffman, Daniel. *Poe Poe Poe Poe Poe Poe Poe.* Garden City, NY: Doubleday, 1972.

Ketterer, David. *The Rationale of Deception in Poe.* Baton Rouge: Louisiana State UP, 1979.

Kirkland, James. " 'The Tell-Tale Heart' as Evil Eye Event." *Southern Folklore* 56 (1999): 135–47.

Pitcher, Edward W. "The Physiognomical Meaning of Poe's 'The Tell-Tale Heart.' " *Studies in Short Fiction* 16 (1979): 231–33.

Poe, Edgar Allan. "The Tell-Tale Heart." *Collected Works of Edgar Allan Poe*. Ed. Thomas Ollive Mabbott. Cambridge: Harvard UP, 1978. 789–99.

Prichard, James Cowles. *A Treatise on Insanity and Other Disorders Affecting the Mind*. London: Sherwood, Gilbert, and Piper, 1835.

Silverman, Kenneth. *Edgar A. Poe: Mournful and Never-Ending Remembrance*. New York: HarperCollins, 1991.

HOW TO
WRITE ABOUT
EDGAR ALLAN POE

WRITING ABOUT POE: AN OVERVIEW

"**B**ELIEVE NOTHING you hear, and only one half that you see," Poe wrote in "The System of Doctor Tarr and Professor Fether," a tale in which a man visits an insane asylum known for its modern methods, only discovering at the end that the people he thought were the doctors are really the patients, who have taken over the asylum and locked up the staff.

To read Poe is to enter a realm of uncertainty. Little can be confidently decided, including—even on the most basic level—what his work is all about. There is likely no other author of Poe's prominence about whom so little consensus exists. Theories have come and gone, and today we are probably more unsure than ever.

Our confusion may be just what Poe was aiming at, for he delighted in mystery and concealment. He invented the detective story. He loved cryptograms and other puzzles. He enjoyed hoaxes and published quite a few. And his tales frequently address the subject of writing that is deliberately designed to "mystify."

The narrator who complains that some rival is posing as him on closer inspection may himself be the real imposter. The character who insists he is not mad but sounds as if he is may have a very good reason for pretending to be. Poe's stories themselves may be impostures. That gruesome horror story appears from some perspectives to be a parody, from others a murder mystery. The newspaper article about the first trans-Atlantic balloon crossing is completely made up. The story that seems to be a careful scientific account of an experiment in hypnotism ends in gross-out humor. In short, the one thing you can be sure of with Poe is that you cannot be sure.

The following advice may be in order, then, for those intending to write about Poe's work:

1. Search beneath the surface. Poe is a sophisticated writer. If something looks simple, look again.
2. Suspect a con. When a writer hoaxes as much as Poe does, you should never be too sure that he is really in earnest.
3. Focus on style, construction, design. Poe did not just pen short stories; he helped define the genre. He was fascinated by the "how" of writing, and he loved to experiment—and play—with form and structure.
4. Leave space for ambiguity. Baffling us is what Poe does. It is natural to try to pierce the confusion, to solve the mystery. But to write well about Poe, you should also write about the confusion itself, for this as much as anything is what his work is about.

Perspectives in Poe criticism

Scholarly criticism of Poe's work may be arranged into separate groups reflecting different perspectives. One approach involves psychological analysis, in which characters and events are viewed as representing conflicts within the human mind. The black cat in the story of that title may be seen as representing the main character's conscience, which he would like to destroy but which comes back to oppress him, finally leading him to reveal his crime. Some readers believe that Roderick Usher is brought to mental collapse by unacceptable feelings for his sister. The way figures in such stories haunt their respective narrators suggests the way unconscious feelings weigh on human beings' consciousness.

Another type of Poe scholarship centers on the unreliability of his first-person narrators. These characters typically struggle to make sense of their experiences, but the reader finds their explanations unconvincing. Their logical approach is insufficient, these tales seem to say, to account for their experiences. This perspective places Poe in the romantic tradition, which insists that an imaginative faculty is needed to truly apprehend the world. The inadequacies of the narrators' accounts may be interpreted in other ways as well. Perhaps the characters are hiding the truth from themselves; perhaps they are concealing wrongdoing from the authorities.

More recent criticism reads Poe's work in the context of his life and times, particularly in relation to the literature and the literary market-place of antebellum America. Critics read Poe against the background of his literary ambitions, the popular culture, and the economic conditions under which he worked. Some view Poe's tales in the light of his desire both to appeal to a mass audience and to set himself above it. Others see them as commenting on the literary forms they appear to take.

Poe, the Man

Perhaps what is most important about Poe as a person is what is not true, for much of the public holds an image of him that is far off the mark. Contrary to a slanderous biography that was written soon after Poe's death and became the standard source on Poe for many years, Poe did not at all resemble the madmen who people his most famous tales.

To his contemporaries, Poe appeared not as some dark and lonesome figure but as an accomplished man of letters, known for his wit. Besides writing fiction and poetry, he was editor of a succession of literary magazines and one of the foremost reviewers of his day. He was covetous of success, and though he did not attain the eminence that he believed his talents deserved, neither did he labor in obscurity. He was conspicuously resentful of the success of others and engaged rival authors in literary battles that roiled the world of the literati.

He struggled desperately against poverty for much of his adult life, and he does appear to have had a drinking problem (an affliction that hardly makes him unusual). At the end of his life his efforts were bent toward finding a woman of means to marry and gaining financial backing for a new literary magazine that he hoped to publish.

It was literature, not ghosts, that consumed Poe, and to the world of literature he contributed a body of work that has shocked, thrilled, delighted, and perplexed readers by the millions, influenced generations of writers—and in immeasurable degree changed the art of writing.

TOPICS AND STRATEGIES
Themes

In writing about themes in Poe's literature, you must steer carefully between two common errors. On the one hand, an essay should not merely identify a common theme observable in one or more works. To observe that certain of Poe's tales concern the power of the unconscious mind is merely to state the obvious. You need to be more specific—and yet not too specific. An essay should also avoid the error of reducing the theme of a literary work to a simple message. It is better to think, and write, of Poe's works as raising issues and ideas than as demonstrating some point.

To write an excellent essay on theme requires, first and foremost, repeated careful readings of the work or works. Try to identify as many details as possible that relate to the chosen theme, from the thoughts and actions of characters to elements of the setting to specific words and phrases. In most Poe tales, these myriad elements form not a single idea but a complex web of ideas. You should not immediately begin to simplify the web. Instead, tease out the varied strands of meaning. If some elements suggest one thing and others suggest something slightly different, or if some elements may be read in more than one way, instead of fixing on one idea you can describe the simultaneous presence of several. Only in this way can an essay do justice to the richness of the work.

Sample Topics:

1. **The unconscious mind:** Poe's characters often seem driven by internal forces that they can neither comprehend nor control. Discuss ways that his tales or poems depict the working of the unconscious mind.

   Many tales are read by many readers as studies of the working of the unconscious. Poe's characters often appear haunted by ghosts or other specters, which may be interpreted as representing unconscious forces. To write an essay along these lines, examine the descriptions of the spectral character and its behavior, as well as the personality of the main character, to explain the nature of the psychological conflict. What, in view of the outcome of the tale, is the result of this conflict?

Unconscious feelings are also revealed in hallucinations and other dreamlike imagery in Poe's work.

2. **Crime and punishment:** Crimes, both actual and implied, figure prominently in Poe's work. Discuss how his tales present human wrongdoing, how we attempt to deal with our crimes, and the toll they exact from us.

Within this category are many good essay topics. First, consider the crimes. In some tales murders are admitted; in others they are suggested. What is the motive for the murder? If the tales are viewed metaphorically, what is the main character attempting to kill?

What are the effects of the crime? What happens to the murderer, either in temporal or psychological terms? Some of Poe's characters are, or appear to be, mad. Does the character's madness lead him to commit the crime, or does his guilt drive him mad? Or is his madness a strategy to avoid acknowledging guilt? Avoid making easy judgments on these matters. In "The Cask of Amontillado" Montresor's apparent pride in the cleverness of his crime may mask powerful misgivings that are only hinted at. Conversely, the narrator of "The Black Cat" expresses extreme remorse yet appears to see himself more as victim than villain. Poe's treatment of these themes is richly ambiguous; a good essay will capture that richness.

3. **Wealth and class:** Issues related to money and social position lie just below the surface of many of Poe's tales. What does his work suggest about the roles that wealth and class play in human life?

In some stories the main character is a man of wealth; in others he is a man of former high estate now in reduced condition. How important is wealth to these men, and in what way? Are they fueled by greed, acquisitiveness, and a desire for luxury, or rather by envy, resentment, and a desire for superiority over others? Are there indications that wealth is more important to them than they acknowledge? Is the issue of wealth straightforwardly presented or is it referred to only obliquely? What does this treatment suggest about the effects wealth exerts in our lives?

Character

Writing about character can be similar to writing about theme. Poe's characters are complex. Many are conflicted, and therefore to write about them adequately you must describe sometimes contradictory elements in their personalities. Compounding the difficulty, most of the characters narrate their own stories, and there are signs that their accounts are not entirely trustworthy. An essay should not try to minimize the complexity that is such a conspicuous feature of the tales.

Sample Topics:

1. **Guilt:** Many of Poe's characters appear racked by guilt. Discuss the experience of guilt in one or more characters.

   One question that might be explored is the source of the guilt. Is the character suffering remorse for an actual crime he has committed? Or is there a deeper psychological source for his guilt? In some cases the murder appears to be a response to guilt: an attempt to erase the conscience-like figure that haunts the character.

   The character's account of his experiences may itself be viewed as a response to his guilt. In what ways does his narrative depict the efforts of a person trying to work out anguishing feelings? Or, might the confusion and obfuscation that we see in his account represent an attempt to deny his guilt?

2. **Blindness:** Poe's characters often fail to understand the circumstances and events they experience. Discuss the nature and implications of this blindness.

   Many characters express confusion, amazement at their experiences, and even uncertainty whether certain events actually happened or were merely imagined. Are the characters overwhelmed by extraordinary events or driven into utter confusion by the psychological pressures they face? Do they fail to understand because their viewpoints are too rationalistic? Or do they fail to understand because they do not want to face the truth? Does William Wilson honestly not see that his nemesis is himself? Does the narrator of "The Black Cat" not recognize that his real problem is his wife, not his cat? What truths about themselves are these men unable to face?

3. **The artistic temperament:** Many of Poe's narrators have artistic proclivities. Discuss this dimension of their characters.

Artists are often thought to possess special sensitivities that dispose them to psychological instability or torment. Roderick Usher, Prospero in "The Masque of the Red Death," and other Poe characters have various kinds of artistic interests or imaginative faculties, along with serious personal or psychological defects. Does the character's artistic nature contribute to his disorder, and if so, what is the connection? If the character's artistic endeavors are merely symptomatic of his disorder, what does his art reveal about what is wrong with him?

History and Context

Poe's work is often regarded as centering rather on timeless matters of individual psychology than on the social issues of his day. But every writer is a product of his culture and time. Moreover, as a magazine editor, Poe was professionally attuned to the currents of popular culture. Indeed, his putative preoccupation with bizarre topics generally mirrored the interests of his contemporaries. Therefore, to familiarize oneself with the culture of Poe's day is to open a new window on his work.

Truly immersing oneself in a different culture takes time. A well-regarded book on some aspect of Poe's culture, such as those listed in the bibliography, makes a good starting point (but keep in mind that in a single book you will see only a limited point of view). Armed with a perspective on some aspect of the culture, reread one or more of Poe's works. What features of these works appear in a different light when viewed from this perspective? Your answer to this question can form the basis for an essay, which would present the relevant information you have learned about the period and then explain its bearing on specific features in the tales.

Sample Topics:

1. **The literary scene:** Discuss Poe's work in the context of the literary milieu in which it appeared.

Literary style constantly evolves. An important part of understanding and appreciating an author's work is to view it in relation to that evolution. Poe's work may be considered in relation to the romantic movement that preceded it. What ideas or images do Poe's tales or poems share with the romantic tradition? How do they depart from this tradition?

You might instead consider Poe, as many do, a pioneer of modernism. How do his works seem modern in comparison to those of his contemporaries? What traits does his writing share with today's fiction? If you do not have a broad background in literature, you could consult secondary sources for background on romanticism or modernism. Articles and books on Poe himself should also contain useful information and might point you to specific tales or poems to consider.

A different approach is to view Poe's work in relation to the audience for which he wrote. Today Poe is mainly read by students in English classes, but in his own time his tales ran in magazines and newspapers. He craved a wide audience and at the same time coveted recognition as an exceptional literary talent. How might these potentially conflicting goals have influenced his work? Could his tales be designed to appeal simultaneously to the general public and to a smaller, sophisticated audience? Do they show evidence of such a design?

2. **Capitalism:** The rise of industrial capitalism in the first half of the 19th century remade the very fabric of social life. Discuss how these changes are reflected in Poe's work.

The forces of capitalism created enormous fortunes and at the same time caused drastic social dislocation and unimaginable poverty. Although Poe did not deal with these issues as explicitly as some of his contemporaries, his tales can be read against the background of changes in the class structure and the anxieties these changes occasioned. Changes in fortune are prominent in works such as "The Gold Bug" and "The Cask of Amontillado" and are subtly referred to in "Ligeia," "William Wilson," and numerous other tales.

Nor were writers mere observers of the new capitalist system, but to a great degree they were victims themselves. You might investigate issues of low pay for writers, aggravated by the absence of copyright laws. Another topic is the emergence of a penny press, which allowed authors to reach a huge audience but at the same time subjected them to the tyranny of the marketplace. Numerous books and articles are available that would illuminate these topics and suggest connections to Poe's work.

3. **Science and the paranormal:** Poe's tales frequently concern scientific or pseudoscientific topics. Discuss the appearance of these topics in the context of public interests and attitudes in Poe's time.

Poe lived in a time of rapid advances in science. Electricity and magnetism were matters of great interest and awe, and so were hypnotism and phrenology. Such topics often found their way into Poe's work, but what role they play is open to question. Does Poe's treatment of them suggest a peculiar interest on his part or merely reflect the general interest? Or does Poe's work exploit the popular interest, and if so, to what purpose or effect? By researching how these topics were discussed throughout the media of Poe's time, you can gain a better vantage point for viewing Poe's own handling of the topics.

Philosophy and Ideas

Writing about philosophy involves a pitfall similar to the one connected to theme. You must be careful not to reduce the tale to a philosophical idea. Such ideas may provide a foundation or backdrop for a literary work but usually should not be thought of as a position that the author is trying to promote. In Poe's time, the concept of reason or rationality, particularly in relation to the imaginative and emotive faculties, provided a basic frame of reference, a widely shared way of thinking about the world. Poe's poems and tales may be said to engage or reflect these perspectives; his works may suggest certain ideas. But avoid asserting that this is what a certain tale is about or is saying. A good basic pattern for an essay is to describe the philosophical concepts themselves and then to suggest how elements in the story touch on these ideas.

Sample Topics:

1. **Rationality:** What ideas do Poe's works suggest about the importance and/or limitations of rational thinking?

   The narrator of "The Tell-Tale Heart" insists that the careful rationality of his behavior proves his sanity. Do you agree? The narrators of "The Black Cat," "The Fall of the House of Usher," and "The Pit and the Pendulum" seem to struggle to think rationally about the extraordinary events they recount. Their efforts fail, and one may very well ask whether in the given situations their rational approach is appropriate. Legrand in "The Gold Bug" and the detective Auguste Dupin are more successful, at least in the sense that they achieve their objectives. Are there ways in which their stories also reveal limitations in rationality?

2. **Mystification:** This word, which Poe used as the title of one of his tales, refers to writing that is designed to confuse. Discuss this concept as it appears in one or more of Poe's works.

   We usually think of writing as involving an attempt to communicate. But much of Poe's work centers on the use of writing to conceal, mislead, or simply baffle. Captain Kidd's secret writing in "The Gold Bug" is designed to be unreadable to anyone but himself. The Minister D. in "The Purloined Letter" attempts to disguise a letter so that it cannot be detected. Some of Poe's narrators may be suspected of trying to conceal their true roles in the events they narrate. Many of Poe's writings themselves are hoaxes, while others fill us with uncertainty. Is this a tale of dark psychological conflict or a parody? Are we meant to shudder or laugh? An effective student essay would probably focus on one or two works. What sort of obfuscation is taking place? Is it a means to a larger end, or an end in itself? If the writer/narrator of a tale—or the tale itself—engages in deliberate obfuscation, what might that imply about the goals, nature, and purpose of literature?

Form and Genre

The study of form and genre may well provide the best approach for students seeking to understand Poe's work. His writing shows a fascination with the structure of story and the complex relationship between text and reader. His exploration of these ideas is one of the things that makes him seem so modern. Poe's work helps define the modern short story, yet he delights in undercutting genres, pulling and twisting them into shapes grotesque and arabesque. He takes gothic tales to their emotional limit—and beyond. Is "Ligeia" a serious tale? A parody? Or something like a campfire story or modern horror movie, which is both scary and funny at the same time? Poe's unreliable narrators puzzle us in other ways. How much can we believe of what they say? Are they truly confused or deliberately trying to deceive us? If we cannot believe them, how are we to make sense of their tales?

By puzzling us like this, Poe forces us to consider basic questions not only about the tales in question but about the experience of reading and the nature of literature. What are our expectations as readers? How does literature evoke, manipulate, gratify or thwart these expectations?

Sample Topics:

1. **The gothic and the fantastic:** Most readers know Poe mainly as a writer of "tales of terror," featuring inexplicable, usually horrific events. Discuss Poe's use of this genre.

   Unquestionably, Poe draws freely from the traditional storehouse of gothic effects: the horrific and supernatural, darkness and decay, terror and madness. A key question is how his tales employ their gothic elements. Are they earnest recreations of the genre, or do they in some way extend or perhaps exploit the genre? This question has been strenuously debated and could be considered in relation to any number of Poe's tales. Does the tale bring depth to the gothic by adding a richer psychological dimension? Does it parody the genre? Or does it somehow succeed in being both horrific and comic at the same time? With appropriate textual support, any of these positions might be argued effectively.

Another approach involves distinguishing between two types of gothic tales: those in which supernatural events really do occur and those in which seemingly supernatural events prove to have natural causes. Yet another genre, called the fantastic, straddles these two, leaving a reader unable to decide between supernatural and logical explanations. Many of Poe's tales may be discussed in terms of the ways in which they involve the reader in this choice.

2. **Psychological allegory:** In this genre, characters represent aspects of the human mind. Discuss one or more of Poe's works in relation to psychological allegory.

Typically an essay would discuss what aspects of the mind the various characters represent and what, psychologically, the interaction between them implies. What does the tale suggest about the sources of psychological conflict and its outcome? An essay on this topic should avoid making a simplistic or overly mechanistic analysis, taking instead a richly descriptive, allusive approach.

It is also possible to argue against reading a particular tale as a psychological allegory. Some readers find "William Wilson" too unsubtle and "Ligeia" and "The Fall of the House of Usher" too ludicrously overblown to be serious psychological allegories. To write an essay along these lines, you would first note the tale's resemblance to psychological allegory and then explain the reasons for not viewing it as such. You would then explain the paradox. What ideas are raised or what effect is created by a tale that pretends to fit this genre while subtly undercutting it?

3. **Humor:** Discuss the role of humor in Poe's work: the subjects he finds humor in, the style of his humor, or his use of hidden humor in seemingly serious works.

Although today Poe is not known for his humor, about half of his tales are overtly comical. By reading a number of his less-known tales, you could experience a range of comic styles, including burlesques, parodies and hoaxes. An essay could discuss Poe's comic style as it appears in one or more works or identify an approach or topic that Poe returns to in a number of tales.

Alternatively, you could examine the presence of humor in Poe's seemingly dark tales. What, if anything, is funny in the tale? How do you reconcile the humor with the apparent seriousness? Does the humor reduce the tale to travesty? Or do you find yourself pulled in opposite directions? What might the story be showing about the strange, close relationship between horror and humor? In "Ligeia," for example, two women die slow deaths in a hideous drama of revivification: What is funny about that? Is the horror funny? Or is our readiness to laugh at such stories horrible?

4. **The unreliable narrator:** In what ways do Poe's narrators raise doubts in the reader regarding the accuracy or honesty of their accounts? What effects do these doubts have on the reading of the tales?

Many of Poe's tales are packed with improbable events, self-contradictions, implausible explanations, admissions of uncertainty, and even explicit disclaimers regarding the narrator's credibility. How do you account for these anomalies? Is the narrator overwrought because of the extraordinary events he has experienced? Is his perception distorted by deep psychological forces? Is he in denial, hiding from himself an unwanted truth? Or is he, for guilty reasons, deliberately deceiving us? As a study of form, an essay on this topic would emphasize Poe's method. How does his text manage to present, as it were, two contradictory tales at once: the story the narrator would have us believe and the divergent story—of madness, denial, or duplicity—that we glimpse behind his account?

5. **Mystery:** Discuss one or more of Poe's detective stories or other stories that contain mystery in terms of their textual features and the ideas or themes that they raise.

Poe is credited with inventing the detective story in three tales featuring the brilliant French detective C. Auguste Dupin. How do the plots, characters, styles, settings, and themes of these stories define the genre? Which of these features seem somehow essential to the genre? What vital role does each play, and how do they work together? Which features seem less essential, more peculiar to these specific works?

Other tales may also be read as mysteries. In various ways, stories as diverse as "The Black Cat," "The Gold Bug," and "The Narrative of Arthur Gordon Pym" all invite us to puzzle them out. Our efforts to solve such mysteries raise fascinating issues about the nature and terms of the encounter between the author (or the text) and the reader. What must a story do to initiate and enable the reader's participation? What does the tale demand of the reader, and what in turn does the reader demand from the tale?

Compare and Contrast Essays

It is important when comparing works to maintain a narrow focus. You might compare two works with respect to a common theme or like characters. Comparisons that are too broad tend to read like mere lists of similarities and differences. To avoid this error, ask yourself what makes the comparison interesting or significant. When the similarities are relatively obvious, little time need be spent in pointing them out. It will be more interesting to explore the differences between the similar elements. Possible topics for compare and contrast essays are mentioned below. Subsequent chapters dealing with individual works offer more specific suggestions.

Sample Topics:

1. **Comparing works by Poe:** Discuss significant similarities and differences in two or more of Poe's works.

   Choose a specific basis for comparison. You might compare characters from different tales: narrators who seem confused or dishonest, perhaps, or frail females who suffer and die. You might compare parallel situations, such as deaths, apparitions, or hallucinations, or examine elements of structure or style, such as Poe's sensationalism or unreliable first-person narratives. Many of the topics discussed previously in this chapter lend themselves to compare and contrast essays.

   You might consider in particular Poe's story "How to Write a Blackwood Article." This story, a spoof of the leading literary magazine of the day, provides valuable context for reading Poe, suggesting how his tales of terror, so often taken at face value, might be viewed in a more humorous light. The tale contains a comic recipe for constructing such tales—a recipe that Poe himself seems to follow. The idea of comparing this spoof to "Ligeia" is discussed in the chapter on that work, but the story could be used in relation to other tales as well.

2. **Comparing Poe's tales with works by different authors:** Discuss some aspect of Poe's work by examining it in relation to the work of a different author.

   Poe's work might be compared with a work in a similar genre by another writer of his own time. What features seem to set Poe apart? It might be even more interesting to compare Poe's work to more recent stories, films, or graphic novels. Poe's tales of terror might be compared to a modern horror story, perhaps in terms of their imagery or self-irony. Poe's Auguste Dupin stories may be compared, from a variety of perspectives, with an almost limitless body of subsequent detective fiction. The metafictional quality of Poe's work might also be examined in a comparison with an ironic or self-referential work of today.

Bibliography

Allen, Michael. *Poe and the British Magazine Tradition.* New York: Oxford UP, 1969.

Auerbach, Jonathan. *The Romance of Failure: First-Person Fictions of Poe, Hawthorne, and James.* Oxford: Oxford UP, 1989.

Bloom, Harold. Introduction. *The Tales of Poe.* Ed. Harold Bloom. New York: Chelsea House, 1985. 1–15.

Bonaparte, Marie. *The Life and Works of Edgar Allan Poe: A Psycho-analytic Interpretation.* Trans. John Rodker. 1949. Reprint, New York: Humanities Press, 1971.

Buranelli, Vincent. *Edgar Allan Poe.* Boston: Twayne, 1977.

Carlson, Eric W., ed. *A Companion to Poe Studies.* Westport, CT: Greenwood Press, 1996.

———. *Critical Essays on Edgar Allan Poe.* Boston: G. K. Hall, 1987.

———. *The Recognition of Edgar Allan Poe: Selected Criticism since 1829.* Ann Arbor: U of Michigan P, 1970.

Cassuto, Leonard. *Edgar Allan Poe: Literary Theory and Criticism.* New York: Dover Publications, 1999.

Culler, Jonathan. *Structuralist Poetics.* Ithaca, NY: Cornell UP, 1975.

Davidson, Edward H. *Poe: A Critical Study.* Cambridge: Harvard UP, 1957.

Dayan, Joan. *Fables of Mind: An Inquiry into Poe's Fiction.* New York: Oxford UP, 1987.

Eddings, Dennis, ed. *The Naiad Voice: Essays on Poe's Satiric Hoaxing.* Port Washington, NY: Associated Faculty Press, 1983.

Eliot, T. S. *From Poe to Valery.* New York: Harcourt, Brace and Co., 1948.

Elmer, Jonathan. *Reading at the Social Limit: Affect, Mass Culture, and Edgar Allan Poe.* Stanford, CA: Stanford UP, 1995.

Foucault, Michel. "What Is an Author?" *The Foucault Reader.* Ed. Paul Rabinow. New York: Pantheon Books, 1984. 101–20.

Gruener, Gustav. "Notes on the Influence of E. T. A. Hoffman upon Edgar Allan Poe." *PMLA* 19 (1904): 1–25.

Guérard, Albert J. "Concepts of the Double." *Stories of the Double.* Ed. Albert J. Guérard. Philadelphia: Lippincott, 1967. 1–14.

Halliburton, David. *Edgar Allan Poe: A Phenomenological View.* Princeton, NJ: Princeton UP, 1973.

Hayes, Kevin J., ed. *The Cambridge Companion to Edgar Allan Poe.* Cambridge: Cambridge UP, 2002.

———. *Poe and the Printed Word.* New York: Oxford UP, 1994.

Herdman, John. *The Double in Nineteenth Century Fiction.* New York: St. Martin's Press, 1991.

Hoffman, Daniel. *Poe Poe Poe Poe Poe Poe Poe.* Garden City, NY: Doubleday, 1972.

Irwin, John. *American Hieroglyphics: The Symbol of the Egyptian Hieroglyphics in the American Renaissance.* New Haven, CT: Yale UP, 1980.

———. *The Mystery to a Solution.* Baltimore: Johns Hopkins UP, 1994.

Kennedy, J. Gerald. *A Historical Guide to Edgar Allan Poe.* New York: Oxford UP, 2001.

———. *Poe, Death, and the Life of Writing.* New Haven, CT: Yale UP, 1987.

Ketterer, David. *Edgar Allan Poe: Life, Work and Criticism.* Fredericton, Canada: York Press, 1989.

———. *The Rationale of Deception in Poe.* Baton Rouge: Louisiana State UP, 1979.

Lawrence, D. H. *Studies in Classic American Literature.* 1923. Reprint, New York: Penguin, 1971.

Levy, Maurice. "Poe and the Gothic Tradition." *ESQ* 18 (1972): 19–29.

Lowell, James Russell. *Fable for Critics.* New York: G. P. Putnam, 1891.

May, Charles E. *Edgar Allan Poe: A Study of the Short Fiction.* Boston: Twayne, 1991.

Mooney, Stephen L. "The Comic in Poe's Fiction." *American Literature* 33 (1962): 433–41.

Moss, Sydney P. *Poe's Literary Battles: The Critic in the Context of His Literary Milieu.* Durham, NC: Duke UP, 1963.

———. *Poe's Major Crisis: His Libel Suit and New York's Literary World.* Durham, NC: Duke UP, 1970.

Muller, John P., and William J. Richardson, eds. *The Purloined Poe.* Baltimore: Johns Hopkins UP, 1988.

Ostrom, John Ward. "Edgar A. Poe: His Income as a Literary Entrepreneur." *Poe Studies* 15 (1982): 1–4.

Pahl, Dennis. *Architects of the Abyss: The Indeterminate Fictions of Poe, Hawthorne, and Melville.* Columbia: U of Missouri P, 1989.

Peeples, Scott. *Edgar Allan Poe Revisited.* New York: Twayne, 1998.

Poe, Edgar Allan. *Collected Works of Edgar Allan Poe.* Ed. Thomas Ollive Mabbott. Cambridge, MA: Harvard UP, 1978.

———. *Edgar Allan Poe: Essays and Reviews.* Ed. G. R. Thompson. New York: Library of America, 1984.

————. *The Letters of Edgar Allan Poe.* Ed. John Ward Ostrom. 2 vols. Cambridge, MA: Harvard UP, 1948.

————. *Marginalia.* Ed. John Carl Miller. Charlottesville: UP of Virginia, 1981.

————. *The Works of Edgar Allan Poe.* Ed. James Harrison. New York: AMS Press, 1965.

Quinn, Arthur Hobson. *Edgar Allan Poe: A Critical Biography.* New York: Appleton-Century-Crofts, 1941.

Quinn, Patrick F. *The French Face of Edgar Poe.* Carbondale: Southern Illinois UP, 1957.

Regan, Robert, ed. *Poe: A Collection of Critical Essays.* Englewood Cliffs, NJ: Prentice Hall, 1967.

Reynolds, David S. *Beneath the American Renaissance: The Subversive Imagination in the Age of Emerson and Melville.* Cambridge, MA: Harvard UP, 1988.

Rosenheim, Shawn. *The Cryptographic Imagination: Secret Writing from Edgar Allan Poe to the Internet.* Baltimore: Johns Hopkins UP, 1997.

Rosenheim, Shawn, and Stephen Rachman, eds. *The American Face of Edgar Allan Poe.* Baltimore: Johns Hopkins UP, 1995.

Silverman, Kenneth. *Edgar A. Poe: Mournful and Never-Ending Remembrance.* New York: Harper Collins, 1991.

————, ed. *New Essays on Poe's Major Tales.* Cambridge: Cambridge UP, 1993.

Sova, Dawn B. *Edgar Allan Poe, A to Z: The Essential Reference to His Life and Work.* New York: Facts On File, 2001.

Tate, Allen. "Our Cousin, Mr. Poe." *The Man of Letters in the Modern World: Selected Essays: 1928–1955.* London: Meridian Books, 1957. 132–45.

Thomas, Dwight, and David K. Jackson, eds. *The Poe Log: A Documentary Life of Edgar Allan Poe, 1809–1849.* Boston: G. K. Hall, 1987.

Thompson, G. R. *Poe's Fiction: Romantic Irony in the Gothic Tales.* Madison: U of Wisconsin P, 1973.

Thompson, G. R. and Virgil L. Lokke, eds. *Ruined Eden of the Present: Hawthorne, Melville and Poe: Critical Essays in Honor of Darrel Abel.* West Lafayette, IN: Purdue UP, 1981.

Todorov, Tzvetan. *The Fantastic: A Structural Approach to a Literary Genre.* Trans. Richard Howard. Ithaca, NY: Cornell UP, 1970.

Weiner, Bruce I. "Poe and the *Blackwood's* Tale of Sensation." *Poe and His Times: The Artist and His Milieu.* Ed. Benjamin Franklin Fisher IV. Baltimore: Edgar Allan Poe Society, 1990. 45–65.

Whalen, Terence. *Edgar Allan Poe and the Masses: The Political Economy of Literature in Antebellum American.* Princeton, NJ: Princeton UP, 1999.

Wilbur, Richard. "The House of Poe" (The Library of Congress Anniversary Lecture, May 4, 1959). Reprint, *The Recognition of Edgar Allan Poe,* ed. Eric Carlson. Ann Arbor: U of Michigan P, 1966. 255–77.

Woodberry, George E. *The Life of Edgar Allan Poe.* 2 vols. New York: Biblo and Tannen, 1928.

Online Resources

Campbell, D. "Edgar Allan Poe." Retrieved 18 April 2007. <http://www.wsu.edu/~campbelld/amlit/poe.htm>.

"Edgar Allan Poe." *American Literature on the Web.* Retrieved September 25, 2006. <http://www.nagasaki-gaigo.ac.jp/ishikawa/amlit/p/poe19ro.htm>.

"Edgar Allan Poe." *The Cambridge History of English and American Literature.* Eds. W. P. Trent, K. Erskine, S. P. Sherman, and C. Van Doren. New York: G. P. Putnam's Sons, 1907–21. *Bartleby.com.* Retrieved 18 April 2007. <http://www.bartleby.com/226/index.html>.

"Edgar Allan Poe." *The Edgar Allan Poe Society of Baltimore.* Retrieved January 20, 2007. <http://www.eapoe.org/works/index.htm>.

"Edgar Allan Poe." *The House of Usher.* Retrieved 18 April 2007. <http://www.houseofusher.net/>.

"Edgar Allan Poe." *The Internet Public Library.* Retrieved 18 April 2007. <http://www.ipl.org/div/litcrit/bin/litcrit.out.pl?au=poe-10>.

"Edgar Allan Poe." *PoetryFoundation.org.* Retrieved January 20, 2007. <http://www.poetryfoundation.org/archive/poet.html?id=81604>.

"Edgar Allan Poe." *Project Gutenberg.* Retrieved January 20, 2007. <http://www.gutenberg.org/browse/authors/p#a481>.

Ehrlich, Heyward. "A Poe Webliography." *Poe Studies: Dark Romanticism* 30 (1997): 1–26. Retrieved 18 April 2007. <http://newark.rutgers.edu/~ehrlich/poesites.html>.

Pridmore, Donna J. "Edgar Allan Poe (1809–1849)." *LiteraryHistory.com.* Retrieved 18 April 2007. <http://www.literaryhistory.com/19thC/Poe.htm>.

Van Dine, S. S. "Twenty Rules for Writing Detective Stories." 1928. Retrieved May 23, 2007. <http://gaslight.mtroyal.ab.ca/vandine.htm>.

"LIGEIA"

READING TO WRITE

"**H**ERE THEN," shrieks the narrator at the end of "Ligeia," "can I never be mistaken—these are the . . . eyes of . . . the LADY LIGEIA!"

Are they? The reader must decide. If you believe that Ligeia truly comes back from death, then you must conclude that this is a tale of the supernatural. If, on the other hand, you believe that the narrator only imagines Ligeia's return, then this is a story about some kind of madman, a man completely overcome by grief or perhaps experiencing a drug-induced hallucination. Another possibility is that the narrator is deliberately deceiving the reader with a load of supernatural nonsense and talk of madness to hide the truth about the death of his wife. In this case, the story would be a mystery. You might even decide that he is kidding, spinning a tale so preposterous and overblown that it can only be a parody. And again you might decide that the story leaves you undecided, that by design it holds you suspended, unable to choose between opposing interpretations.

Such is the design of "Ligeia" that it may be read in any of these ways. In fact, all of these interpretations have been advanced by at least one professional scholar.

To decide for yourself, you must read the text closely and repeatedly. Consider what the narrator says that makes sense and also the many things he says that do not seem to make sense. How credible is the story of the return from the dead? Exactly how grief-stricken, how mad, how drug addicted do you believe the narrator to be? What about the overall tone of the tale: Does it frighten you? Puzzle you? Or is it so over the top that it makes you want to laugh?

Consider these questions in relation to the climactic ending of the tale. The narrator's second wife has died, and he is alone with her body in his bedroom, which is fantastically decorated with bizarre figures and Egyptian sarcophagi. He says he has been smoking opium. He suddenly hears a low sob and soon finds a slight flush of color return to his wife's body. He tries to revive her (he does not say how), but the body once again becomes cold and pale. This happens repeatedly: Each time, the body comes more fully to life but then sinks back into a seemingly more final death. Finally, near dawn, the body stirs again:

> And again I sunk into visions of Ligeia—and again, (what marvel that I shudder while I write?) *again* there reached my ears a low sob from the region of the ebony bed. But why shall I minutely detail the unspeakable horrors of that night? Why shall I pause to relate how, time after time, until near the period of the gray dawn, this hideous drama of revivification was repeated? . . . .
>
> The corpse, I repeat, stirred, and now more vigorously than before. The hues of life flushed up with unwonted energy into the countenance—the limbs relaxed. . . . I could at least doubt no longer, when, arising from the bed, tottering, with feeble steps, with closed eyes, and with the manner of one bewildered in a dream, the thing that was enshrouded advanced bodily and palpably into the middle of the apartment.
>
> I trembled not—I stirred not—for a crowd of unutterable fancies connected with the air, the stature, the demeanor of the figure, rushing hurriedly through my brain, had paralyzed me—had chilled me into stone. . . . One bound, and I had reached her feet! Shrinking from my touch, she let fall from her head the ghastly cerements which had confined it, and there streamed forth, into the rushing atmosphere of the chamber, huge masses of long and disheveled hair; *it was blacker than the wings of the midnight!*

The writing is indeed thrilling. It sweeps us away, if we let it, into a kind of abandoned terror tinged with glee. If we stand back from it, however, even for a moment, our reaction is apt to change. The hair "blacker than the wings of the midnight," the narrator "chilled into stone," the wild image of a tottering corpse returned to life, its white shroud and raven hair streaming in specially designed indoor wind—do they seem a little clichéd, a little silly? The passage is so over the top: Can we really take it seriously? Are we meant to do so?

Moreover, the first of the quoted paragraphs peculiarly calls attention to the writing of the story itself. Indeed, it does so in a way that seems to disparage the writing. The narrator's statement that he shudders as he writes is clever. He seems to mean that the memory of the event makes him shudder, but the words can be interpreted to mean that it is his writing itself that makes him shudder. This idea is reinforced two sentences later, when he speaks of the "hideous drama of revivification," a phrase that again can be read as referring to either the events he is describing or his narrative itself. In short, just at the point of its highest emotion, the text invites us to stop and view it critically: to adopt exactly that stance that is likely to lead us to conclude that the passage is too overblown to be taken seriously.

So in the rest of the man's story, if we examine it critically we find much to consider, if not criticize. Some of what he says is simply unbelievable. (He does not remember Ligeia's name.) Some is ludicrous. (Ligeia's eyes were "even fuller than the fullest of the gazelle eyes of the tribe of the valley of Nourjahad.") And a great deal is cryptic.

After evaluating the entire story in this manner and identifying the specific elements that contribute to your reaction, you might arrive at an overall response to the tale. Does one emotion predominate? Is your feeling mostly one of terror? Humor? Puzzlement? Your answer, supported by reasons, provides the foundation for an essay. Many readers, it should be said, experience more than one of these emotions. In that case, it is necessary not only to show where and how the text elicits these reactions but also to generate a theory about how these effects work together.

The topics discussed below provide more specific frameworks within which such ideas can be developed.

TOPICS AND STRATEGIES
Themes

"Ligeia" appears to tell the story of a woman who either comes back to life or is believed by her husband to do so. These two possibilities suggest the tale's most prominent themes: either a serious inquiry into the possibility of reincarnation or a terrifying depiction of the power of the mind to create dark and terrifying visions.

Sample Topics:

1. **Reincarnation:** Taken at face value, the story tells of a woman who returns to life in another woman's body. Many people strongly believe in the transmigration of souls, while others at least entertain the possibility. What does the tale suggest about this concept?

The idea receives particular mention in connection with Ligeia's studies and the description of her lingering death. What enables her to accomplish this extraordinary feat? Is it her character, her special knowledge, or something in her circumstances? You should also consider the words of the headnote, which the narrator returns to repeatedly. Going beyond what the statement says, how is it used in the tale?

It is also possible to consider the theme metaphorically, rather than literally. Could Ligeia's reappearance suggest a broader idea of rejuvenation, or could it perhaps mock such an idea?

2. **Grief, remorse, and madness:** Read as a psychological tale, "Ligeia" traces the descent into hallucinatory madness of a man bereaved of his wife. What ideas does the story suggest about the causes and effects of the narrator's mental collapse?

Ligeia's death appears to produce in the narrator a progressive decline, which includes his bizarre, obsessive decorating; his remarriage to a woman he hates and subsequent abuse of her; his abuse of drugs; and finally his descent into hallucination. To what extent should these behaviors be considered effects of his grief, and to what extent do they contribute to his decline? The death of a spouse does not drive most people mad. Is there something in the narrator's character that leads to his decline?

Or are his circumstances responsible? Some of his statements in the first half of the tale suggest that his marriage was not as idyllic, nor his love for Ligeia as boundless, as he means to suggest. Does he experience feelings of guilt or remorse in relation to Ligeia? Do such feelings contribute to the devastation people experience at the death of those they love?

Character

In approaching the characters in the story, as in approaching the tale itself, readers face choices in interpretation. If you take the narrator's story at face value, you are likely to view him as a rather normal man reacting understandably to exceptional circumstances. You are likely to view Ligeia as anything but a normal woman.

If you believe instead that the narrator only imagines Ligeia's reincarnation, the focus shifts dramatically. In that case, you should consider what has led him to his delusional state. The focus shifts again if oddities in the way he tells his story lead you to suspect that he is hiding something. In this case, you must read between the lines for clues that either he or Ligeia or both may be quite different than they appear.

Sample Topics:

1. **The narrator as hallucinatory:** Many readers believe that Ligeia does not return in reality but only in the narrator's imagination. Describe the nature and causes of the narrator's madness.

   The narrator himself suggests several factors. He describes his grief at the death of Ligeia as crushing and acknowledges an opium addiction. Is the narrator's madness merely the result of these external factors? Or is there something in his character that renders him susceptible to these forces? For example, is there something that predisposes him to a belief in the supernatural or to drug use?

   You might also consider whether guilt plays a role, a possibility that is described in the previous question about the theme of grief, remorse, and madness.

2. **The depiction of Ligeia:** The narrator describes Ligeia in such extravagant, abstract, and metaphorical ways that it is difficult to see her as a flesh and blood person. Discuss the description of this character, its effect on readers, and its role in the tale.

First note how odd and unreal are the narrator's descriptions of Ligeia. What is it about these descriptions that makes them so strange? Next, what effects do they have on the reader? Do they help make Ligeia herself seem mysterious and unusual and in that way strengthen the notion that she could come back to life?

Alternatively, does the unreality reflect instead on the narrator? Does it make you wonder why he does not speak more plainly about the woman he loves? Does it make you wonder "what she was really like"? Was she passionate or placid? Did she genuinely love him or not? Is it possible, behind the narrator's hyperbole, circumlocution, and self-contradiction, to trace a consistent pattern of hints about her?

Finally, Ligeia is unambiguously depicted as learned, and some readers see her as an allegorical figure. An essay could discuss her character as representing learning or some particular branch of learning. Such an essay would offer a theory about how this idea of her fits into a story of rejuvenation or reincarnation, either real or imagined.

3. **The narrator's relationship to women:** What ideas does the story suggest about the narrator's attitudes and behavior toward his two wives?

You might begin by examining the narrator's description of his relationship with Rowena. He says outright that he hated her. What do you make of his further statement that she "dreaded the fierce moodiness of [his] temper" and that this gave him "pleasure"? What is he revealing about himself?

As for Ligeia, he insists that he loved her, but if you read between the lines, is there evidence that their relationship was as tumultuous as his relationship with Rowena? What might you infer from the way he keeps slipping words like *strange* and *startling* into his long rhapsodies on Ligeia's beauty? Why do those descriptions somehow sound so absurd? Whose passions is he actually referring to when he describes Ligeia as "violently a prey to the tumultuous vultures of stern passion"?

Form and Genre

Genre offers a particularly important approach to "Ligeia," for as discussed in the "Reading to Write" section, the tale admits a wide variety of different readings. Each reading implies a different genre.

Writing on this topic involves considering the conventions that characterize a given genre and discussing how well they seem to fit the tale. You may conclude that the tale fits one genre very well and explain why. Alternatively, you might discuss the way the tale defies categorizing, how it seems to fit more than one genre. Questions to consider include how the construction of the tale enables it to be read in different ways and why a tale would be designed in such a way.

Sample Topics:

1. **"Ligeia" as ghost story:** Discuss the story's use of elements commonly found in ghost stories.

   One traditional form of ghost story tells of a person who is killed (or whose body is violated after a natural death). The climax of the story details the slow approach of the ghost to exact its revenge on the perpetrator. In what ways does the plot of "Ligeia" conform to this model? What plot elements are different or of questionable similarity? If Ligeia is thought of as returning to exact revenge on the narrator, what conjecture could be made about her reason—and on what textual evidence?

   Besides considering the plot, an essay should review additional features that "Ligeia" shares with other ghost stories, including its grotesque setting, vivid descriptions of the narrator's sensations, electrifying diction, and even extreme punctuation.

2. **"Ligeia" as explained gothic:** This term is applied to stories with events that seem to be supernatural but ultimately are explained in terms of natural causes. How does "Ligeia" fit this genre?

   One way to explain Ligeia's appearance at the end of the tale is to regard it as a figment of the narrator's imagination. You could then examine the conditions that lead to this hallucination. Obvious places to begin are the narrator's grief at the death of his first wife and his admitted drug use. A deeper examination, however, reveals a pervasive preoccupation with death, clearly observable, for example, in the way he decorates his new home. The narrator suggests that Ligeia was preoccupied with this subject. Did he absorb this interest from her? Or is it possible that he is projecting on her his own lifelong obsession?

3. **"Ligeia" and the fantastic:** This term refers to a genre that lies between the supernatural and the explained gothic. In the fantastic, parts of the story suggest a supernatural explanation, while other parts seem explainable in terms of the situation and psychology of the main character. Ultimately, the reader is left uncertain which interpretation to adopt. Explain how "Ligeia" fits this genre.

An essay on this topic would draw on ideas from both of the two preceding topics. The bulk of such an essay would detail the presence in the story of both explained and unexplained elements. What elements of the story incline you to believe that Ligeia really does appear at the end? Which elements lead you to think that the narrator is only imagining things? The essay might then discuss the effect on the reader of this irresolvable uncertainty.

4. **"Ligeia" as humor:** While much of the tale is horrifying, some parts seem ridiculous. Discuss the role humor plays in "Ligeia."

This essay should identify the parts of the tale that seem humorous and use these examples to explain the nature of the humor. Many readers view the story as a parody, a work that evokes laughter mainly by taking the conventions of the genre and exaggerating them to the point of absurdity. Typical elements of gothic fiction are described in the first question above. Which of these elements can "Ligeia" be seen as parodying?

We also laugh sometimes at horror stories (and movies) that are not intended as parodies. What makes us laugh? Is it that, even though they mean to scare us, they are so obvious, so overblown, or so tacky that we laugh at them? This unintended humor is not parody, but camp. Or do the works somehow mock themselves? If so, what is the nature of this self-parody, and how is it accomplished? Does "Ligeia" fit into one of these categories? More than one? An essay could discuss these categories and your reasons for placing the tale in one category or another.

Finally, what might the story be saying about the strange, close relationship between horror and humor? Two women die slow deaths in this "hideous drama of revivification": What is funny about that? Is the horror funny? Or is our readiness to laugh at such stories horrible?

5. **"Ligeia" as mystery:** A man's wife or perhaps both of his wives die under mysterious circumstances. Can the tale be read as a murder mystery?

A mystery story typically includes murder, suspects, alibis, and a solution. The essayist must decide whether these ingredients are present in "Ligeia." The unexplained nature of the two wives' illnesses and the suggestion of poison in the case of Rowena's death lead some readers to suspect murder. The suspect could only be the narrator. Does his tale of drug addiction and hallucination sound like an alibi? Do some of his statements seem incredible, contradictory, or evasive?

Of equal importance, a mystery presents a puzzle for the reader to solve. Does the reader of "Ligeia" try to puzzle out the story? An essay that pursues this question could delve interestingly into the ways that the tale does or does not resemble a mystery.

Compare and Contrast Essays

As its name implies, a compare and contrast essay involves a discussion of both similarities and differences. In "Ligeia," the narrator emphasizes the differences between his two wives. These differences should be given due account, but you should also look closely for similarities between the women and between their deaths. An essay might even consider why the narrator chooses to emphasize the differences over the similarities.

Sample Topics:

1. **Comparing Ligeia and Rowena:** How are the narrator's two wives depicted, and what role does this depiction have in your response to the story?

   A difficulty in considering these characters is that neither emerges as a lifelike figure. Indeed, an essay might focus less on the characters themselves than on the narrator's portrayal of them. What does he reveal about Ligeia, and what does he reveal about Rowena? What does he not reveal about either woman? What effect do his portrayals have on your attitudes toward each woman? What do the portrayals reveal about him?

2. **Comparing the two wives' deaths:** Both of the narrator's wives die of unidentified wasting diseases, yet in some ways the deaths seem quite different. Discuss the similarities and differences and what they suggest about the two women and the narrator's relationship to them.

   The circumstances surrounding the two deaths, and certainly the narrator's stated feelings about them, seem to differ markedly. An essay on this topic should note these apparent differences. However, when the relevant parts of the tale are read very closely, striking similarities appear. You might particularly consider the poem that Ligeia composes. What is she describing in this poem? If it is her own death, then even more similarities to Rowena's death may be seen. Finally, if the two women's deaths are found to be very similar, what might that mean in terms of the overall story that is being told?

   You might also compare one or both of the deaths in this tale to the death or deaths of women in other Poe tales. In fact,

the death of a beautiful woman was one of Poe's favorite top-
ics. A few tales to consider are "The Assignation," "Berenice,"
"Morella," "The Fall of the House of Usher," and "The Black
Cat."

3. **Comparing "Ligeia" with "How to Write a Blackwood Article":** The latter, a send-up by Poe of the leading literary magazine of the day, was published just two months after "Ligeia."
Compare the two pieces and discuss what the comparison
suggests in terms of how "Ligeia" can be interpreted as a comic
tale.

The "Blackwood" article has two parts. In the first, a magazine
editor provides a list of rules for constructing tales "full of
taste, terror, sentiment, metaphysics, and erudition"—in other
words, tales very much like Poe's. The second part presents
an aspiring writer's attempt to translate Blackwood's advice
into fiction: a ridiculous story about a woman who gets her
head stuck between the hands of a clock. An essay could begin
by identifying the many passages in "Ligeia" that conform to
Blackwood's advice. The essay could then draw comparisons
between elements in the woman's silly story and similar elements in "Ligeia." Are the corresponding elements equally
ridiculous? If not, what makes one ridiculous and the other
serious?

Bibliography for "Ligeia"

Basler, Roy P. "The Interpretation of 'Ligeia.'" *College English* 5 (1944): 363–72.

Dayan, Joan. *Fables of Mind: An Inquiry into Poe's Fiction.* New York: Oxford
UP, 1987.

Gargano, James. "Poe's 'Ligeia.'" *College English* 23 (1962): 337–42.

Griffith, Clark. "Poe's 'Ligeia' and the English Romantics." *University of Toronto
Quarterly* 24 (1954): 8–25.

Jordan, Cynthia. "Poe's Re-vision: The Recovery of the Second Story." *American
Literature* 59 (1987): 2–3.

Lauber, John. "'Ligeia' and Its Critics: A Plea for Literalism." *Studies in Short
Fiction* 4 (1966): 28–32.

Leverenz, David. "Poe and Gentry Virginia." *The American Face of Edgar Allan Poe*. Ed. Shawn Rosenheim and Stephen Rachman. Baltimore: Johns Hopkins UP (1995): 210–36.

Matheson, Terrence J. "The Multiple Murders in 'Ligeia': A New Look at Poe's Narrator." *Canadian Review of American Studies* 13 (1982): 279–89.

Shi, Yaohua. "The Enigmatic Ligeia/'Ligeia.'" *Studies in Short Fiction* 28 (1991): 485–96.

Schroeter, James. "A Misreading of Poe's 'Ligeia.'" *PMLA* (1961): 397–406.

Tate, Allen. "Our Cousin, Mr. Poe." *The Man of Letters in the Modern World: Selected Essays: 1928–1955*. London: Meridian Books, 1957. 132–45.

Todorov, Tzvetan. *The Fantastic: A Structural Approach to a Literary Genre*. Trans. Richard Howard. Ithaca, NY: Cornell UP, 1970.

West, Muriel. "Poe's 'Ligeia.'" *Explicator* 22 (1963): 15.

"THE FALL OF THE HOUSE OF USHER"

READING TO WRITE

In "The Fall of the House of Usher" a man tells an extraordinary story of visiting his friend in a gloomy, decaying mansion and witnessing the friend's descent into madness, the wasting away of the friend's sister, and her burial in a tomb beneath the house—and ultimately, one dark and stormy night, her horrifying return from the grave, the death of both brother and sister, and the collapse of the house. In encountering such a tale, and certainly in planning to write about it, you must first decide how much credence to give it.

One choice is to accept the narrator's account at face value and to conclude that events, including Madeline's supernatural escape from her tomb, occur essentially as the narrator describes them. A second option is to reject the narrator's version of events, just as you might refuse to believe a man in real life who told us such a story. In this case, you would shift your attention to the narrator himself. Why is he telling such a preposterous story? Is he mad? Is he lying? Or perhaps he is joking. Perhaps his tale is a spoof or the kind of story told around campfires, which, although ostensibly scary, elicits as many laughs as chills.

Having adopted a basic attitude toward the tale, you will read accordingly. If you view the story as a genuine tale of terror, you will focus on the settings, the atmospherics, the descriptions of the characters' sensations. If you take a more skeptical approach, you will search for references to Roderick's—and the narrator's—mental state. If you see the story as a spoof, you will look for evidence of mimicry and exaggeration.

This process does not follow a straight line. It goes back and forth between what you have read before and what comes after and between your initial ideas and the new evidence you find. You may start with a certain viewpoint and look for elements in the text that support this view. But do not ignore elements that seem to conflict. Instead, constantly try to incorporate new ideas, seeking to build a reading that is consistent with as much of the text as possible. Some examples of this reading process can be applied to one excerpt from "Usher." The following passage appears in the part of the story in which Roderick and the narrator descend into the underground vault to bury Madeline.

> At the request of Usher, I personally aided him in the arrangements for the temporary entombment. The body having been encoffined, we two alone bore it to its rest. The vault in which we placed it (and which had been so long unopened that our torches, half smothered in its oppressive atmosphere, gave us little opportunity for investigation) was small, damp, and entirely without means of admission for light; lying, at great depth, immediately beneath that portion of the building in which was my own sleeping apartment. It had been used, apparently, in remote feudal times, for the worst purposes of a donjon-keep, and, in later days, as a place of deposit for powder, or some other highly combustible substance, as a portion of its floor, and the whole interior of a long archway through which we reached it, were carefully sheathed with copper. The door, of massive iron, had been, also, similarly protected. Its immense weight caused an unusually sharp grating sound, as it moved upon its hinges.

Looking at the details of this passage, ask yourself, Why is the story telling you this? How does it make you feel? What does it make you think? Most readers would agree that the passage as a whole gives a spooky feeling. A good reader, however, should be able to explain quite specifically what makes the descriptions so effective. First, there are many sense words: You can *see* the "half-smothered" torches, *feel* the "damp" and the weight of the "massive iron" door, and *hear* the "sharp grating sound" it makes. The information that the vault had been a dungeon makes it seem more fearful. It also makes us think of Madeline as a prisoner—someone who is alive and cannot get out, rather than just a dead body. (You might also consider the idea that Roderick too seems like a prisoner.) The statement that the vault lies immediately beneath the narrator's bedroom brings the tomb and all its creepiness closer to the living men. Observations of elements such as these in the story would be useful in an essay that discussed "Usher" as a genuine tale of terror.

Your response to other parts of the passage may be quite different. The vault had once been used to store gunpowder, and the ceiling and floor were lined with copper. This fact is more surprising than the fact that the vault had been a dungeon, and its import is less apparent. It perplexes us more than it chills us. If it is mentioned, it must be significant, but in what way? Keep it in mind, however, and try to connect it with other parts of the story. Are there other points that seem more perplexing than horrifying? If so, you might want to piece them together to argue that the story is not just out to scare you; it has some further goal.

You will also need to connect other details of the passage to the rest of the story. The passage states that the vault, when closed, admits no air and that the weight of the door is "immense" and grates when it turns. In the paragraph following the one quoted, the narrator adds that the coffin lid is screwed down and the door secured from the outside. On the one hand, these details prepare the reader for the terrifying sounds that the men later hear or believe they hear. At the same time, they discredit the narrator's assertion that Madeline physically clawed her way back from a premature burial. Not even a healthy person could survive eight days in an airless chamber and then remove a screwed-down coffin lid and open a massive door bolted on the outside. Some readers will choose to believe that Madeline escapes by supernatural means (or that it is her ghost that appears in the doorway), while others might use the details of her burial to show that the narrator is not to be trusted.

In this passage, then, there is evidence to support a variety of seemingly conflicting interpretations. Do other passages similarly invite such divergent readings? If so, you might argue that the tale has been designed either to provide different experiences for different readers or to hold readers suspended, not knowing what to think. You might decide, instead of discussing just one interpretation of the story, to examine the simultaneous presence of conflicting readings. This approach could lead to a complex but very sophisticated essay.

TOPICS AND STRATEGIES
Themes

"The Fall of the House of Usher" traces the deterioration and ultimate destruction of Roderick, his family, and his house. The themes of the story cluster around this basic core. To identify specific themes, you might search through the story and list ideas associated with decay: Roderick's fear, his madness, his unorthodox artistic endeavors, his relationship with his sister. One strategy involves focusing on a topic and describing what the story seems to say about it. An equally valid approach is to consider how the story depicts these various states. Consider the various images in the story: the decaying house, Roderick's bizarre painting, the figure of Madeline, and the underground tomb. What connections can be made between these images and the themes of madness, fear, imagination, rationality, art, and death?

Sample Topics:

1. **Psychological identity:** How does the story represent the duality of the human mind or self?

   By depicting Roderick and Madeline as twins with intertwined fates, the story invites us to view brother and sister as two parts of one psychological whole. An essay on this topic would draw on descriptions of the two characters to describe what each side of this self is like, as well as how the parts interconnect. Clearly this organism is unhealthy, and an effective essay would go on to discuss, in terms of the two selves, what has gone wrong.

2. **Terror:** At one point in the story, Roderick predicts that he will "perish" of fright, and the ending of the story suggests that he does. At the same time, the tale as a whole may be viewed as the story of two men who work themselves into a state of almost paralyzing fear. What ideas does "Usher" offer about the nature and sources of fear in our lives?

   A basic overall approach to this topic is to analyze Roderick's fear—his most conspicuous feature—and try to apply your findings to the condition of mankind in general. Roderick's condition is a hard knot to unravel. There are hints that he harbors a guilty secret. Readers who find these hints strong enough may argue that Roderick's fears (and ours) are driven by guilt. Other readers find it impossible to trace Roderick's condition to any specific source. Has it no real object at all, then? Has he created it himself? Do we all, in a sense, do what Roderick has done? Or again, do we all do to ourselves what the reader of "Usher" does: search in vain for an objective cause that does not exist? It is also worthwhile to explore the role of the narrator. He says that Roderick's condition "infected" him, and he shares Roderick's terror at the end of the tale. Does he just get carried away by the gloom and the storm, or do humans infect each other with their deepest fears?

3. **Imagination:** The story discusses in detail Roderick's painting and poetry, his esoteric tastes in music and philosophy. What stance does the tale seem to take toward artistic and intellectual pursuits?

An essay might survey the discussion of intellectual matters in the tale or focus in detail on one of Roderick's pursuits, such as his phantasmagoric painting. Particular attention should be given to the narrator's remarks about the effects of Roderick's activities and/or the relationship between these activities and other events in the tale. Does imagination enhance life, does it mirror life, or does it distort life and divorce us from natural reality?

4. **Dissolution and decay:** How does the decay and ultimate collapse of the physical house correspond to the degeneration of the Usher family?

To write an essay on this topic, look at the many passages in the story that describe the decaying of the house, the decline of the family, and the deteriorating mental or physical health of its two remaining members. Also, consider Roderick's poem

"The Haunted Palace," which seems to compare his mind to a house. What ideas do these passages supply regarding the nature and causes of this decay?

Character

A good starting point for writing about character is to choose one person and one point of interest about him or her. In the case of Roderick Usher, many ideas spring to mind. He seems to be going mad. What is the nature of his madness, or what is its cause? He is depicted as artistic, and eccentrically so. What do you learn about the nature of his artistry, and how does this relate to the extraordinary events of the story? The tale refers to a special affinity between Roderick and Madeline (and also between Roderick and the narrator); explaining such connections could also make an interesting essay. Nor should you restrict your thinking to the leading characters. In "Usher" the narrator himself deserves close attention, and particularly an exploration of how credible he is.

Sample Topics:

1. **Roderick and his house:** How is the house in the story used as an image of Roderick's mental state?

   Numerous passages personify the house, beginning with a reference in the first paragraph to the "vacant and eye-like windows." Elsewhere the house is compared to the Usher family and to Roderick in particular; the collapse of the house at the end of the story obviously mirrors Roderick's mental collapse. In addition, Roderick's poem "The Haunted Palace" provides an extended comparison between ruined palace and Roderick's failing mind. A paper on this topic would analyze such descriptions and discuss how they apply to Roderick's mental state.

2. **Roderick as artist:** The story describes in detail Roderick's artistic and intellectual pursuits. Describe Roderick as an artist and intellectual.

   Writing on this subject would involve examining the parts of the story that detail Roderick's artistic endeavors. A thoughtful paper would not merely describe Roderick as artist but also try to relate this aspect of his personality to the rest of the story. How, for example, is his art connected to his madness? Is it a result, or sign, of the madness? An attempt to escape from it? Or part of the cause?

3. **The double:** The story describes Roderick and Madeline as mysteriously connected, almost as if they were two parts of one person. How might these two characters represent the two sides of one personality?

To write on this topic, you would identify the many places in the text where connections are drawn between the two characters, as well as examine how the text characterizes each. In what ways does one sibling complement the other? In what ways are they dependent on each other? If you focus on Roderick as the main character, does the relationship between brother and sister provide a useful image for the psychological struggle that is raging within Roderick?

4. **The unreliable narrator:** How believable is the narrator's version of events? What in his words or actions makes him credible or not credible?

If someone in real life told you what the narrator tells you, you would not believe him. What *would* you believe? The man admits that he was crazy with fear; perhaps he imagined these things. You might believe that Roderick's madness, the creepy house, and Madeline's death and burial combine to terrify the narrator into believing the impossible. Alternatively, could he be lying? He does equivocate quite often, using phrases such as, "It may have been" or "I thought I heard." Sometimes he actually contradicts himself. But why would he lie? What could he be hiding? Perhaps the text provides some clues.

Form and Genre

The literary name for horror stories like "Usher" is *gothic*. This was one of the earliest fictional genres, and it was wildly popular for at least a half-century beginning around 1765. Works such as Horace Walpole's *The*

Castle of Otranto, Ann Radcliffe's *The Mysteries of Udolpho,* and Matthew Gregory Lewis's *The Monk,* characterized by crumbling medieval castles, ghostly apparitions, unexplained noises, and such, were the best sellers of their time. Early in their development, gothic stories split into two groups. In supernatural gothics the ghosts or vampires are real. In explained gothics the spectral events turn out to have a rational explanation. (Perhaps, for example, someone deliberately arranged the apparitions in order to scare away the rightful owner of the house and inherit it himself.) A good genre study of "Usher" would not only identify the parts of the story that conform to gothic conventions but also try to suggest the functions these conventions serve. Why is it stormy? Why is the heroine so often fair and dressed in white?

You might also ask whether Usher presents these conventional elements in earnest or is more tongue in cheek? Gothic stories were already the object of parody long before "Usher" appeared in 1839. Parody works through a combination of imitation and exaggeration. Is "Usher" a parody? How can you decide?

Sample Topics:

1. **"Usher" as gothic:** In what ways does "Usher" conform to the conventions of gothic fiction?

   As discussed above, you should identify common elements of gothic fiction in the story and discuss their effects on readers. Decide whether the tale is an example of the supernatural or the explained gothic. The central question is whether Madeline truly escapes from her tomb or whether the two men only imagine it. You should take a stand on this question and supply evidence from the story to support it.

2. **"Usher" as parody:** Some readers believe that "The Fall of the House of Usher" is a parody of the gothic genre. Do you agree or disagree? Explain your answer.

   An essay on this topic would weigh the effect of the gothic elements of the story on the reader, especially the scene in which the narrator reads a novel to Roderick and the men hear, or imagine they hear, noises in the house that coincide with what happens in the novel. Are these elements genuinely frightening, or are they so clichéd and exaggerated that they make you want to laugh? (A reader familiar with the gothic genre would recognize that specific elements in "Usher" have been lifted from two of the most famous gothic novels of all time, *The Castle of Otranto* and *The Mysteries of Udolpho*. This fact could support the view of "Usher" as a parody.) It is also possible to write about the story as something between a serious gothic and a parody: a work that combines the horrifying and the comic.

3. **"Usher" as mystery:** The story leaves many readers more puzzled than horrified. In what ways does the tale resemble a mystery? What might be the solution?

If you reject the narrator's version of events, then naturally you will wonder what really happened. In addition, the tale raises a number of questions. Is Roderick hiding a secret? What causes Madeline's illness? Is she buried prematurely? What causes the house to collapse? A good paper on this topic would try to identify what makes the story feel like a mystery, whether or not you try to solve the mystery.

Compare and Contrast Essays

One way to write an essay on a work of literature is to compare elements in different stories, discover either similarities or differences between them, and then comment on those discoveries. A good essay would not just list similarities and differences but analyze and consider what purpose those similarities or differences might serve. To formulate a thesis for an essay, ask how the two things are related to each other. Do they corroborate, extend, complicate, contradict, correct, or debate each other?

Sample Topics:

1. **Comparing gothics:** "The Fall of the House of Usher" and "Ligeia" are perhaps Poe's two most elaborate gothic tales. Compare and contrast these stories in terms of their content and style.

An essay on this topic would examine the gothic elements in the two stories, such as their dark and threatening settings, the breathless descriptions of characters' feelings of terror, and the plots involving women coming back from death (or appearing to do so). Where you find similarities between the two tales, you might ask whether these indicate a preoccupation of the author or merely a reliable strategy for creating suspense or terror. When differences emerge, you might ask how they produce different effects.

2. **Comparing mental breakdowns:** Roderick Usher is one of a number of characters in Poe's works who suffer some kind of psychological breakdown. Compare Roderick's mental decline with that depicted either in another Poe tale or in "The Raven."

You might choose two or more works for comparison. You could focus on similarities and differences in the causes of the declines (internal or external) or in the process of disintegration. It would be interesting to consider style, too: not only what is being depicted but the manner in which it is presented.

3. **Comparing Roderick's painting to Fuseli's:** The narrator compares Roderick Usher's painting to the work of Henry Fuseli. How would you compare the description of Roderick's painting of a vault with "The Nightmare" or some other work by this painter?

This would be a speculative essay, in that Roderick's painting may only be imagined, based on the narrator's description. Although the composition of the two paintings is completely different, comparisons may be made about their styles and the feelings and ideas they engender. It is also possible to make such speculative comparisons to a work or works by some other painter.

4. **Comparing descriptions of the house:** Compare the narrator's evocative descriptions of the exterior and interior of Ush-

er's house with Roderick's own descriptions in his poem "The Haunted Palace."

An essay on this topic would describe the similarities and differences between the two men's descriptions. It might consider what these features suggest about the mental and emotional state of the two men. Do the two men view events differently, and if so, is this difference reflected in their descriptions? It should be noted that Usher's house is often viewed as representing his mind; an essay might well consider what the two men's descriptions reveal about their conception of Roderick's mental state.

Bibliography for "The Fall of the House of Usher"

Brown, Gillian. "The Poetics of Extinction." *The American Face of Edgar Allan Poe.* Ed. Shawn Rosenheim. Baltimore: Johns Hopkins UP, 1995. 330–44.

Carlson, Eric W, ed. *The Fall of the House of Usher.* Columbus, OH: Merrill, 1971.

Dayan, Joan. "The Dream of the Body." *Fables of Mind: An Inquiry into Poe's Fiction.* New York: Oxford UP, 1987. 199–200.

Fisher, Benjamin Franklin IV. "Playful 'Germanism' in 'The Fall of the House of Usher': The Storyteller's Art." *Ruined Eden of the Present: Hawthorne, Melville, Poe.* Ed. G. R. Thompson and Virgil L. Lokke. West Lafayette, IN: Purdue UP, 1981. 355–74.

Haggerty, George E. "Poe's Gothic Gloom." *Gothic Fiction/Gothic Form.* University Park: Pennsylvania State UP, 1989. 81–106.

Kaplan, Louise. "The Perverse Strategy in 'The Fall of the House of Usher.'" *New Essays on Poe's Major Tales.* Ed. Kenneth Silverman. Cambridge: Cambridge UP, 1993. 45–64.

Pahl, Dennis. "Disfiguration in 'The Fall of the House of Usher,' or Poe's Mad Lines." *Architects of the Abyss: The Indeterminate Fictions of Poe, Hawthorne, and Melville.* Columbia: U of Missouri P, 1989. 3–24.

Peeples, Scott. "Poe's 'Constructiveness' and 'The Fall of the House of Usher.'" *The Cambridge Companion to Edgar Allan Poe.* Ed. Kevin J. Hayes. Cambridge: Cambridge UP, 2002. 178–90.

Quinn, Patrick. "'Usher' Again: Trust the Teller!" *Ruined Eden of the Present: Hawthorne, Melville, Poe.* Ed. G. R. Thompson and Virgil L. Lokke. West Lafayette, IN: Purdue UP, 1981. 341–53.

Thompson, G. R. "Poe and the Paradox of Terror: Structures of Heightened Consciousness in 'The Fall of the House of Usher.'" *Ruined Eden of the Present: Hawthorne, Melville, Poe.* Ed. G. R. Thompson and Virgil L. Lokke. West Lafayette, IN: Purdue UP, 1981. 313–40.

Woodson, Thomas, ed. *Twentieth Century Interpretations of "The Fall of the House of Usher."* Englewood Cliffs, NJ: Prentice Hall, 1969.

"WILLIAM WILSON"

READING TO WRITE

"**W**ILLIAM WILSON" offers a study in how readers try to make sense of what they read. Making sense of this tale is no easy task. On a literal level, it is almost impossible to state what actually happens in the story. In some cases there is not enough hard information. What happens, for example, at Bransby's school when the narrator goes late at night to visit his rival? Something seems to happen—something important—but the tale does not specify what. In other cases, extraordinary, unbelievable coincidences raise doubts whether what is being suggested is true.

Many readers give up the search for a literal meaning and instead make sense of the tale as an allegory, that is, a literary creation in which characters and objects stand for things or ideas. In "William Wilson" the two men are most often viewed as representing two parts of the human self or human mind: the selfish will and the conscience, perhaps, or in Freudian terms, the id and the superego. The rivalry between the two Wilsons figures the struggle between these two parts of the psyche. This conflict might be considered from a number of perspectives. You might focus on the struggle itself: the feelings that the narrator describes of rivalry and competition, of the other's attempt to overmaster him, or of being pursued. Alternatively, you might explore the possible causes of the conflict. What clues does the tale give about when, where, how, and why the rivalry developed? Or working in the opposite direction, you might consider the destructive ending of the story and draw out what possible meanings this may imply.

Another approach consists in examining the form of the tale itself. While some parts seem allegorical, others seem concrete and literal, and still others seem more like mystery than anything else. An essay could discuss the presence of these seemingly conflicting elements in the tale.

To observe in concrete terms how readers may try to make sense of "William Wilson," consider the ending of the tale. Immediately before the passage that follows, the narrator drags his opponent into an empty room, defeats him in a one-sided swordfight, and stabs him repeatedly. He then hears someone at the door and runs to lock it. When he returns, he says, everything is changed:

> A large mirror,—so at first it seemed to me in my confusion—now stood where none had been perceptible before; and, as I stepped up to it in extremity of terror, mine own image, but with features all pale and dabbled in blood, advanced to meet me with a feeble and tottering gait.
>
> Thus it appeared, I say, but was not. It was my antagonist—it was Wilson, who then stood before me in the agonies of his dissolution. His mask and cloak lay, where he had thrown them, upon the floor. Not a thread in all his raiment—not a line in all the marked and singular lineaments of his face which was not, even in the most absolute identity, *mine own.*
>
> It was Wilson; but he spoke no longer in a whisper, and I could have fancied that I myself was speaking while he said:
>
> *"You have conquered, and I yield. Yet, henceforward art thou also dead—dead to the World, to Heaven and to Hope! In me didst thou exist—and, in my death, see by this image, which is thine own, how utterly thou hast murdered thyself."*

The passage contains a number of features that can be found throughout the story. One is the emotional, overwrought language. The narrator's "extremity of terror," the features "dabbled in blood," the dashes, the italics—these all raise the emotion to a feverish level. The narrator writes in this excited manner throughout the tale. Perhaps this kind of writing reflects the intensity of his fears about the "other Wilson." Alternatively, the writing could be considered from the standpoint of the reader. Is it an attempt by Poe to play on readers' emotions? Could it be a ploy by the narrator to keep readers from asking hard questions about what the man is saying?

The passage also presents a dizzying array of contradictions and questions. There appears to be a mirror, but there is not. There appears to be a second man, but the passage suggests there is really only one. The rival speaks, but the narrator "fancies" that it is he himself who is speaking. The rival does not speak in a whisper, but we have been told that he was unable to speak above a whisper. A review of the entire tale will produce dozens of such contradictions and puzzles. Are the rivals at Bransby's school brothers or not? Were the two boys similar, as the narrator claims? If so, why was this never observed by the other students? It may be impossible to answer such questions conclusively, but a good reading of the story should try to account for the presence of so much confusion. Does the confusion reflect the narrator's inability—or unwillingness—to understand what is really happening to him? Does the confusion of the tale, like the maze that is Bransby's school, represent the complexity of the mind? Or is the narrator, perhaps, not really as confused as his account suggests?

Thematically, the passage seems to sum up the idea that the two William Wilsons are one. If you think of the rival as the man's conscience, as many readers do, then the apparent murder seems to be the man's attempt to free himself from this conscience that he feels is hounding him. The final quotation seems to say that in killing his conscience the man has killed his own soul. This is a common reading, but many readers object. The man writing, or telling, the story is doing so after the swordfight is over and done. Yet as he writes he shows signs of having a very strong conscience. How can this be if he has killed his conscience? It seems as if our every attempt to make sense of the story is blocked. Could that be part of its design?

TOPICS AND STRATEGIES
Themes

The fundamental conflict in the tale is most commonly read as a battle between two halves of one self. Growing out of this perspective, the most prominent themes are related to psychological issues such as the divided self, denial, and so on.

To write on such topics, gather details that describe each of the two Wilsons and use these details to construct a working theory of what these two characters represent. Next consider their interaction: the antagonism, the imitation, the pursuit. Here again specific details should be collected to formulate specific ideas. The topics listed below provide examples of how to narrow your focus and move from the ideas in the story to what these ideas suggest about some aspect of the human condition.

Sample Topics:

1. **The divided self:** How does the story represent the duality of the human mind or self?

Viewing the two William Wilsons as two halves of one person leads naturally to a consideration of how these two sides interact. Writing on this theme would involve examining the many parts of the text that deal with the competition between the two Wilsons. What, specifically, does this competition suggest about ways that human beings experience conflict within themselves?

2. **Denial:** This theme grows out of the theme of the divided self. One strategy of the mind for dealing with conflict within itself is to try to deny the existence of disturbing, conflicting impulses.

The narrator frequently claims not to understand who the other Wilson is. This could make a good starting point for a paper on denial. Such a paper could also discuss the attempts of the narrator to flee from his rival. It could discuss the motivations of the narrator for denying his alter ego as well as his strategies for doing so, and it might go on to suggest how these story elements are related to the real-life experience of denial.

3. **Conscience:** The headnote to the story refers to "conscience grim." How does the tale represent the human conscience?

Many statements and events in the tale can be found to support the view that the narrator's alter ego is his conscience, which is trying to make him do the right thing. An essay on this topic might discuss the dual nature of the conscience: On the one hand, it is trying to make the narrator a better person; on the other hand, it fills the narrator with dread. What ideas does this give about the nature of conscience in our own lives?

4. **Identity:** This tends to be a very broad topic, and the first thing you should do is narrow its focus.

One approach is to consider what gives the narrator his sense of identity. His wealth and status seem important to him: He refers to these privileges all the time. He also speaks frequently about his "evil nature," about how bad a life he has lived; he almost seems to brag about it. Is it just that he needs to feel unique, whether that means being the richest or being the most evil? What do these ideas suggest about the role that people's self-image plays in their lives?

Character

The section on themes suggested ways to write about the story's depiction of the ideas of the divided self, guilt, and so forth. The allegorical nature of the tale promotes such abstract thinking. Yet it is also possible to think about William Wilson as an individual person. What is this man like, and what in the story shows it?

Sample Topics:

1. **The narrator's guilt:** The narrator seems to regard his alter ego as something like his conscience. He bitterly resents this figure and seeks to escape from it. Would you agree or disagree that the tale depicts a man tormented by his conscience?

You might focus on the deep resentment the narrator feels toward his "rival." The many examples provided in the story might suggest that the narrator is a man racked by feelings of guilt. However, he says that he has lived a life of depravity. If that is true, then his conscience would not seem to be very strong. An essay could take either position, or it could try to reconcile the conflict. Is the narrator's bad behavior a kind of rebellion against his domineering conscience? Or is it that he has no conscience at all but keeps insisting how bad he feels as a way of getting sympathy from people and perhaps a pardon for his misdeeds?

2. **Self-recognition:** Characters are thought to grow if they come to realize something about themselves that they did not see before. Does the narrator grow in this way?

It is possible to write an essay arguing that the story shows a character who continually tries to deny or defeat his "other self." At the end he succeeds, but in doing so he realizes that he has killed himself. Such a realization could be viewed as a sign of growth.

The tale contains a paradox, however. The man's story, which is being told after all the events it describes have taken place, is filled with self-blame. Where is this self-blame coming from, if he has killed his conscience? An interesting essay might first explain this paradox and then offer a solution. If the man has killed his conscience, then perhaps all his self-blame is a pretense, designed to win forgiveness for his behavior. Or, since the character is very good at imitation, could it be that the two Wilsons have changed places? Could the profligate Wilson be the dead victim and the conscience Wilson the one who is left alive?

3. **The narrator's unreliability:** The narrator seems to be deceiving himself. Is he also trying to deceive us?

To write on this topic, you would have to search carefully for signs of not just self-delusion but outright deception. The narrator often seems evasive, as at the start of the tale, when he declines to give his true name and says he will not tell the full story of his later life. His description of key events is also less than direct. He often describes episodes in very dramatic terms, without ever describing what actually happened. He also admits that in some respects his version of events is different from what his schoolmates observed. After collecting evidence of possible deceit, you must consider motive. Why might the narrator wish to deceive his reader? Has it to do with his life of "unpardonable crime"?

History and Context

Always be judicious in making connections between a work of literature and the life and times of its author. On the one hand, it is inevitable that an author's concerns will show up in his or her work. On the other hand, it must be remembered that the author is writing a work of fiction. A good essay on contextual topics describes the background issue factually and suggests points of connection to the story. Such an essay would probably not try to make one-for-one connections between story and context; rather, it should use the context to provide an enriched appreciation of the story while always striving to do justice to the story in its own right.

Certain elements of "William Wilson" seem to connect quite directly to prominent issues in Poe's life. One of these is money, along with the related matter of social position. Poe was raised in luxury but lived his adult life in poverty. (He attended a private school in England headed by a man named Bransby.) Poe's letters and other writings express bitter resentment toward his foster father and others in comfortable circumstances. Speaking more generally, Poe lived during a time of economic upheaval and anxiety. In the throes of the Industrial Revolution, wealth was shifting, poverty was rising. Writers, too, faced new commercial conditions and pressures. Against this background, an essay could explore the class antagonisms that are expressed in "William Wilson."

Sample Topics:

1. **Class:** Discuss issues of wealth and social class in the context of Poe's life or times.

The story is set at a succession of exclusive schools, Eton and Oxford being two of the most famous schools in England, that are associated with nobility. The narrator makes much of his station in life, referring repeatedly to matters of wealth and station. He also appears to rise rapidly in station, under somewhat mysterious circumstances. An essay could relate these turns of fortune to the dramatic changes that came with the rise of capitalism in Poe's time, as described in the introduction to this section and in the "History and Context" section of the chapter "How to Write about Poe."

Another approach is to relate the tale to Poe's personal history. Much information is available concerning the resentment he harbored at the loss of support from his foster father. How might William Wilson's expressed lust for wealth and his antagonism toward his wealthy and powerful rival reflect Poe's own preoccupations?

2. **Plagiarism:** Imitation, the deliberate copying of the clothes and behavior of another, runs throughout "William Wilson." In literature, imitation often means plagiarism, an issue that was of consuming interest to Poe.

In an age before copyrights were in force, plagiarism was a vital economic concern for Poe. It was also a deeply personal one. As a literary critic, he focused much effort and attention on charges of plagiarism, which he leveled at a number of prominent authors. An essay on this topic would involve research into plagiarism issues in Poe's time and career and particularly his extended attacks against Henry Wadsworth Longfellow. An essay could explore the connections between the issues Poe raised and the elaborate imitation in "William Wilson."

Form and Genre

Deciding what type of story one is reading—what genre—might seem to be a simple task. But with Poe's tales the decision is not easy at all, and

"William Wilson" is no exception. Trying to decide can be both frustrating and fascinating.

At first the story appears to be a psychological allegory, in which characters and events represent aspects of the human psyche. Much of "William Wilson" seems to fit this form well, and an essay could present the case for an allegorical reading.

Alternatively, an essay could explore the reasons for rejecting such a reading. For one thing, as many critics have argued, the allegory the story presents is rather simple and superficial. Moreover, the questions and contradictions that pervade the tale tend to make the reader wonder not just what events mean but what actually happens in the tale. In this regard, the story seems more like a mystery than an allegory. Other elements read like a melodrama. A good essay could examine the ways in which the story fits into different genres at the same time. A creditable essay would demonstrate how Poe's tale "bends genres"; an exceptional essay would formulate and present a theory suggesting what literary purpose such genre bending might serve.

Sample Topics:

1. **Psychological allegory:** Many readers consider "William Wilson" a psychological allegory in which the two characters represent two parts of the human psyche. Is it one, or does it only pretend to be?

   A paper on this topic would first explain the idea of psychological allegory and then describe how "William Wilson" fits this form. This discussion would include what the two Wilsons represent as well as what is represented by their interaction throughout the tale and especially at the end. It might also consider the narrator's telling of the tale. Why does he seem so mystified, and why does his account seem to leave such gaps? What does this suggest about the psychological struggle he experiences?

2. **Genre bending:** Does the tale fit more than one genre at a time?

This idea was discussed in the introduction to the "Form and Genre" section. An essay on this topic could survey the different genres the tale seems to fit: psychological allegory, ghost story (or tale of the "fantastic"), mystery, and melodrama. Rather than argue that the tale really represents one of these genres or another, the essay could explore the idea that the story is designed to cross or straddle more than one genre.

3. **The doppelganger:** This term refers to a ghostlike double of a living person. The doppelganger is a popular feature of horror and fantastic fiction, from Robert Louis Stevenson's *Dr. Jekyll and Mr. Hyde* to Stephen King's *The Dark Half.* Describe Poe's use of this literary device.

   After introducing the concept of the doppelganger, an essay would probably trace how the story creates and uses this character. How does the tale identify him as representing the main character and at the same time give him something of a separate identity? Above all, it is the nature of a doppelganger to be shadowy and spooky. His presence is in some way disturbing to the narrator. How does the story make Wilson's double so spooky? Why thematically does it do so?

4. **Deliberate confusion:** Literature often leaves readers uncertain about what really happened, whether events were real or only imagined, and more. Sometimes this feeling of uncertainty seems to be part of the work's design.

   For this topic, you would first note what is confusing in the story. This might include questions about the identities of the characters, about what really happens in the tale, and about what happens at the end. Is the narrator's doppelganger real or imaginary? Are the events real or imagined? Is the tale just an allegory, or can the events be read as actually occurring? Next you would want to make the case that the story is not just difficult but confusing by design. Try to think of a reason: What artistic effect does the story achieve by leaving readers so uncertain?

Compare and Contrast Essays

"William Wilson" invites essays of comparison. The most obvious approach is to compare the two Wilsons. Other ideas are described below.

Sample Topics:

1. **Comparing the two Wilsons:** Discuss the similarities and differences between the two rivals.

   An essay on this topic would probably center on the idea that the two characters represent two sides of the human personality or psyche. The speaker portrays himself as the willful, profligate side, while his rival appears to represent something like his conscience. This much seems simple. You could go on to probe details of the characters and their interaction, such as Wilson's speech impediment and the two men's relative social standing.

2. **Comparing key scenes:** Wilson confronts his alter ego in four key scenes: the late-night visit at Bransby's, the early-morning intrusion at Eton, the card game at Oxford, and the final masked ball. Compare some or all of these scenes.

   Planning an essay on this topic would begin with a scrutiny of the details of the scenes in question. What patterns emerge? It is noteworthy that the encounters become longer and more dramatic as the story progresses. Does the nature of their interaction change over time? Or does the basic pattern of interaction remain consistent but keep growing more elaborate?

3. **Comparing doubles:** The presence of a character who appears to be a counterpart or mirror of another character is common

in literature. In gothic and horror fiction the double is often a shadowy and spooky figure. Compare the motif of the double in "William Wilson" to that in another work of fiction.

Of the innumerable novels and tales that contain doubles, a few to consider are *Dr. Jekyll and Mr. Hyde* by Robert Louis Stevenson, "The Double" by Fyodor Doestoevsky, "The Jolly Corner" by Henry James, *The New York Trilogy* by Paul Auster, and *The Dark Half* by Stephen King.

An essay could compare the works thematically. What ideas do the doubles suggest in each work? Alternatively, you might compare the works stylistically. How are the doubles introduced in each work, and how are they described? What devices do the two works use to affect the reader's intellectual and emotional responses to the doubles?

Bibliography for "William Wilson"

Bate, Nancy Berkowitz. "I Think but Am Not: The Nightmare of William Wilson." *Poe Studies/Dark Romanticism* (June–December 1997): 27–38.

Bonaparte, Marie. *The Life and Works of Edgar Allan Poe: A Psychoanalytic Interpretation*. Trans. John Rodker. London: Imago Publishing, 1949.

Elmer, Jonathan. "The Prescriptive Right of the Mob." *Reading at the Social Limit: Affects, Mass Culture, and Edgar Allan Poe*. Palo Alto, CA: Stanford UP, 1995. 71–92.

Halliburton, David. "William Wilson." *Edgar Allan Poe: A Phenomenological View*. Princeton, NJ: Princeton UP, 1973. 302–08.

Herdman, John. *The Double in Nineteenth Century Fiction*. New York: St. Martin's Press, 1991.

Hoffman, Daniel. "Seeing Double." *Poe Poe Poe Poe Poe Poe Poe*. New York: Doubleday, 1972. 211–18.

Labriola, Patrick. "Edgar Allan Poe and E. T. A. Hoffman: The Double in 'William Wilson' and 'The Devil's Elixirs.'" *International Fiction Review* (2002): 69–77.

Poe, Edgar Allan. "Henry Wadsworth Longfellow." *Edgar Allan Poe: Essays and Reviews*. Ed. G. R. Thompson. New York: Library of America, 1984. 670–777.

Rovner, Marc Leslie. "What William Wilson Knew: Poe's Dramatization of an Errant Mind." In *Poe at Work: Seven Textual Studies.* Ed. Benjamin Franklin Fisher IV. Baltimore: Edgar Allan Poe Society, 1978. 73–82.

Stern, Julia. "Double Talk: The Rhetoric of the Whisper in Poe's 'William Wilson.'" *ESQ* 40 (1994): 185–218.

Tate, Allen. "The Angelic Imagination." *The Recognition of Edgar Allan Poe.* Ed. Eric W. Carlson. Ann Arbor: U of Michigan P, 1970. 244–48.

"THE MASQUE OF
THE RED DEATH"

READING TO WRITE

"THE MASQUE of the Red Death" is a short, seemingly uncompli-cated story, yet like so many of Poe's tales it can be read in several very different ways.

Most readers view it as an allegory, a story in which characters and objects represent ideas. The Red Death, for example, may be seen as representing death itself, and the clock as representing the inevitable passage of time. Writing about allegory involves interpreting events in the story in accordance with the meanings we have attached to the various story elements. Thus, if the Red Death represents death, then the retreat of Prospero and his guests to their secluded abbey might be interpreted as the attempt of human beings to deny the inevitability of their own mortality.

Alternatively, the story may be read as a dream or perhaps a delusion. An essay could examine those aspects of the tale that make it seem dreamlike. You might then turn your attention to the dreamer, Prospero. What ideas can you form about him based on the nature of his dream or delusion?

Do not fail to appreciate the supreme artistry of this short tale. Its structure, its extraordinary setting, the vivid images it presents and the spellbinding sound of its prose combine to form a work of almost perfect elegance. Any number of fine essays can be written if you focus on some aspect of the story's form or style, describing its effect on readers and how it enhances the tale's overall design.

So artfully is the story crafted that you may choose a passage almost at random and find elements in it supporting any of the ideas and approaches just mentioned. Consider the paragraph that begins by intro-ducing the masqueraders:

> [Prince Prospero] had directed, in great part, the moveable embellish-ments of the seven chambers, upon occasion of this great *fête*; and it was his own guiding taste which had given character to the masquer-aders. Be sure they were grotesque. There were much glare and glitter and piquancy and phantasm—much of what has been since seen in "Her-nani." There were arabesque figures with unsuited limbs and appoint-ments. There were delirious fancies such as the madman fashions. There was much of the beautiful, much of the wanton, much of the *bizarre*, something of the terrible, and not a little of that which might have excited disgust. To and fro in the seven chambers there stalked, in fact, a multitude of dreams. And these—the dreams—writhed in and about, taking hue from the rooms, and causing the wild music of the orchestra to seem as the echo of their steps. And, anon, there strikes the ebony clock which stands in the hall of the velvet. And then, for a moment, all is still, and all is silent save the voice of the clock. The dreams are stiff-frozen as they stand. But the echoes of the chime die away—they have endured but an instant—and a light, half-subdued laughter floats after them as they depart. And now again the music swells, and the dreams live, and writhe to and fro more merrily than ever, taking hue from the many-tinted windows through which stream the rays from the tripods. But to the chamber which lies most westwardly of the seven, there are now none of the maskers who venture; for the night is waning away; and there flows a ruddier light through the blood-colored panes; and the blackness of the sable drapery appals; and to him whose foot falls upon the sable carpet, there comes from the near clock of ebony a muffled peal more solemnly emphatic than any which reaches *their* ears who indulge in the more remote gaieties of the other apartments.

First, read to construct allegorical meaning. The chiming of the clock is a reminder of the inescapable passage of time. It is a black clock that stands in the black and red room and so may be thought to repre-sent not only the passage of time but the inevitable approach of death. The revelers may be thought of as ordinary humans living, as all do, under the shadow of eventual death. Most of the time we ignore the reality of our mortality. Every so often, however, something reminds us. Then we stop our thoughtless pursuits and turn serious—but only for a brief time. Almost at once we push aside unwelcome thoughts and escape again into our activity.

Moving beyond this basic interpretation, examine the text more closely and begin to attach more specific ideas to the many details the passage supplies. The wearing of costumes might suggest that people put on an appearance that hides their true selves. Some of our assumed personas are beautiful, some are bizarre, some disgusting, but all, the passage seems to say, are grotesque. Perhaps it is the very idea of masking our true selves that is grotesque. In addition, in the light coming through the tinted windows, the dancers take on unnatural colors. It seems that not only their costumes but the entire environment they dwell in is artificial. Nor, despite their attempts to be merry, do the revelers seem genuinely happy. The passage says that the dancers "stalked" and "writhed" in and out of the colored chambers. A variety of ideas may be attached to details such as these; there is no one correct interpretation.

The passage, like the tale as a whole, lends itself to other approaches. It refers to the dancers as "dreams" and says that both the furnishings and the costumes were the creation of Prospero. These points, together with the dreamlike quality of the tale itself, invite the reader to view the entire story as either the dream or the delusion of Prospero.

Also manifest in the passage is Poe's powerful prose style, which provides much of the weighty gloom the tale conveys. Readers should note Poe's use of repetition, as in "There were . . . there were" and "much of . . . much of." The repetition of "there were" also leads to the frequent inverting of ordinary word order, as in the sentence, "To and fro in the seven chambers there stalked, in fact, a multitude of dreams." One might argue that such twisting of sentences contributes to the feeling of abnormality that pervades the tale. Through it all, Poe maintains a somber if irregular rhythm in his language. The highly stylized structure and sound give the tale an air of unreality that fits well with both allegory and dream.

TOPICS AND STRATEGIES
Themes

The dominant, unmistakable theme of the story is death or, one might say, human mortality. The withdrawal of Prospero and his guests into the abbey is, in concrete terms, an attempt to escape from the epidemic that is ravaging the land. Metaphorically, these men and women are trying to escape death; naturally, their attempts are doomed to fail. From this starting point, an examination of the tale will turn up a great many details that can be used to explore a whole web of interrelated themes. Such details include not only the action of the story but the descriptions of the frenzied masqueraders, the ghastly decorations, the ebony clock, and the figure of the Red Death.

Sample Topics:

1. **Mortality:** How does the story represent death and human beings' reactions to their own mortality?

   The entire action of the story can be viewed in terms of the attempt by Prospero and his guests to escape death, which is described in horrific terms in the opening paragraph and in somber, final terms at the end. A good essay would take as its starting point the obvious idea that death inevitably triumphs despite all human attempts at escape and would examine in depth the details in the story that suggest the myriad ways humans deal with the reality of death.

   One strategy, escape, is shown not only by the withdrawal into the abbey but also by the masqueraders' frenzied partying. Note, too, their behavior each time the clock tolls the hour, their avoidance of the seventh room, and their reactions to the appearance of the figure of the Red Death.

2. **Crime and punishment:** Some readers see a biblical quality in the tale. How might it be read as a tale of retribution against Prospero and his guests?

An essay on this topic might begin by noting elements in the story that seem biblical. The first paragraph describes the "pestilence," and the prominent mention of blood in the paragraph is reminiscent of the first of the 10 plagues of Israel. The last paragraph says that the Red Death has come "like a thief in the night"—a biblical quotation. This paragraph also gives prominence to the word "fall," and its final sentence sounds biblical indeed. The essay could go on to consider the sins for which Prospero and his fellow revelers might find themselves punished, suggested in the reference in the first paragraph to the lack of aid and sympathy for their fellow human beings.

3. **Masquerade:** How is the idea of masquerade used in the tale? What might the story be saying about masking and pretending?

To begin with, consider the idea of a masquerade in the context of the story. (The word *masque* can be used to mean a mask that one wears or a masquerade ball itself.) Wearing a mask is a way of hiding, and the masked ball can be seen as part of an attempt to hide from death. But masquerading also involves pretending to be what one is not. What issues does the story raise about people playing a part or about the conflict between outward appearance and inner reality?

4. **Dreaming:** In what ways is the story like a dream? What ideas does it present about the nature of dreaming?

An essay on this topic might start by observing the passages in which the idea of dreams and dreaming is expressly stated. You could go on to explore the possibility that the story itself is a dream, pointing out features of the text that give the story a dreamlike feeling. What might these features reveal about the nature of dreams and dreaming? Finally, you might try to make a connection between the theme of dreaming and the theme of mortality.

Character

The characters in "The Masque of the Red Death" are not drawn in life-like detail. Prospero is the only character (except, arguably, the figure of the Red Death) who is given any individuality at all. About him very little is said, but the details the story does offer may be combined to form a coherent concept of him.

The masqueraders conspicuously lack individuality, as is common for characters in an allegory, who may be thought of as representing "every-man." These revelers may be viewed as a group, and inferences about their collective character may be drawn from the group's behavior.

Sample Topics:

1. **Prospero's eccentricity:** In what ways is Prince Prospero depicted as unusual? Why might he be characterized in this manner?

   The Prince (also referred to as a duke) is said to have a "love of the *bizarre*." It is he who is responsible for the unusual design of the rooms of the abbey, its furnishings, and many of the masqueraders' grotesque costumes. An essay on Prospero could examine some of the details of these grotesqueries and might speculate on what they reveal about their creator. Such an essay might go on to suggest a connection between the duke's taste for the bizarre and his attempt to escape death.

   An essay might also explore the idea of Prospero as artificer. Like his namesake, the wizard of William Shakespeare's *The Tempest,* he has created his own world. He can thus be seen as an artist, a dreamer (since the world he creates is removed from the real world), or, in view of how bizarre his world is, a madman.

2. **The revelers:** How are Prospero's guests depicted, and how does this depiction fit the design of the story?

   Although none of the guests are drawn as individuals, an essay could examine the description of the group. It could note their frenzy, their grotesque costumes, their avoidance of the seventh room, their behavior each time the clock tolls the hour, and finally their behavior toward the figure of the Red Death. Most likely you would discuss these attributes of character in allegorical terms—that is, from the standpoint of what this behavior indicates about the reactions of ordinary humans to the knowledge that they must die.

History and Context

The lack of details concerning time and place and the highly stylized story line incline most readers to think of the story more as an allegory or a dream than in terms of actual historical events. It is possible, however, to connect the story to real events in Poe's time and in his life. In doing so, most writers avoid claiming specific connections between elements in the story and real events. Instead your goal as a writer should be to suggest ways in which these contexts can enrich an appreciation of the tale.

Sample Topics:

1. **Virginia Poe's illness:** What connections might be made between Poe's tale and his wife's incurable disease?

   In January 1842 Poe's wife Virginia suffered a lung hemorrhage, spitting up blood; this was a symptom of tuberculosis, the dreaded disease that ultimately killed her, as it had Poe's mother and foster mother. Poe is believed to have composed "The Masque of the Red Death" in March of that year, and it is easy to speculate that his story was influenced by his personal experience. An essay on this topic should probably avoid claiming that Poe was writing about his wife. Instead, it might discuss the ways in which the story captures the emotions that someone might experience if his or her loved one was suffering an incurable disease.

2. **Epidemics:** Deadly epidemics were common in Poe's time. How might this context, with all its attendant fears, help frame a reading of the story?

The Red Death is a fictitious disease, invented by Poe. The name calls to mind the black death, which devastated Europe in the 14th century. A more direct parallel can be drawn to an 1832 cholera epidemic in Paris, during which many balls were given. At one of these, a masquerade, a very tall man appeared dressed as a personification of the cholera. An essay could explore this historical background, but here, as with the matter of Virginia's illness, you should focus primarily on what Poe has created.

Form and Genre

"The Masque of the Red Death" is a highly stylized work. For many readers, the tale's supreme mastery of form and structure is its most noteworthy feature.

Writing about form and structure involves focusing on the literary features of the text. You may describe the tale as an allegory, a dream, a ghost story, or some combination of these genres. In each case, the process is similar. You will need to examine how the story is constructed and how it says what it says. How do these elements conform to the conventions of the genre (or genres) in question?

In addition, many good essays could be written discussing aspects of the structure or the prose style of the tale. A general strategy is to identify and describe a noteworthy feature of the text and explain how it fits the artistic design of the tale.

Sample Topics:

1. **"The Masque of the Red Death" as allegory:** Describe the features of the tale that mark it as an allegory. How would you interpret the allegory?

   Allegories seem literary and figurative in contrast to realistic or literal. In seeking to identify what leads you to read the tale allegorically, you might note the lack of a literal interpretation of events, particularly the appearance of the Red Death, a figure having no tangible form. An essay on this topic might also point out the lack of detail regarding the place and time of the events, the use of a fictitious disease, and the lack of individualized characters.

The overall message of the allegory—the futility of human efforts to deny or escape death—seems obvious. A thoughtful paper would consider more specifically what the tale suggests about the ways in which men and women shrink from the reality of their mortality. Examples might be found in the characters' retreat to an isolated abbey, their grotesque costumes and frenzied partying, their behavior when the clock strikes the hour, their avoidance of the seventh room, and their reactions to the appearance of the Red Death.

2. **"The Masque of the Red Death" as dream or delusion:** The tale contains numerous references to both dreams and madness. How might the story be read as either a dream or a mad delusion?

You might first point out that the masqueraders are expressly referred to as "dreams" and "phantasms" and that the succession of colored rooms seems very dreamlike. What is more, both the costumes and the setting are said to have been created by Prospero himself, a fact that might lead you to view Prospero as the dreamer.

You might also think of this dream as a delusion. The story reveals that some people consider Prospero mad and makes other references to madness, such as the statement that the guests' costumes were "delirious fancies such as the madman fashions." An essay could explain the reasons for reading the tale as Prospero's mad delusion and might go on to make inferences about the nature of his madness.

3. **The setting of the tale:** A large portion of the tale is devoted to a description of the rooms of the abbey and the behavior of the revelers each time the clock strikes the hour. What does this background information contribute to your experience of the tale?

An essay on this topic could take one or both of two approaches. One approach is to discuss what the background details seem to add to the meaning of the tale. It has been suggested, for example, that the seven rooms represent the seven days of the week, the seven deadly sins, or the seven ages of man. The sequence of colors of the rooms also invites varied interpretations. The general meaning of the gigantic ebony clock should be readily apparent. An essay could tease out more specific and subtle ideas by examining the details of the description of both the clock and the revelers' reactions to it.

The elaborate background of the story may also be viewed in relation to the emotional effect it produces on readers. The bizarre design of the rooms contributes to the spookiness of the story. At the same time, the design also piques readers' intellectual interest as they try to puzzle out the significance of the colors and their progression. An essay might explore these paradoxical reactions.

4. **"The Masque of the Red Death" as ghost story:** In its design and its effect on readers, how does the tale resemble popular ghost or horror tales?

You might begin by considering precisely what makes the tale scary. It is not merely the threat of the fatal disease but also the ghastly colored rooms, the frightening costumes, the ominous clock, and so on. Poe is a master of sight and sound, and in this tale is experienced a succession of unforgettable images and dramatic prose.

It is also enlightening to trace the structure of the tale. Like the ghastly rooms of the abbey, the story itself is highly contrived and stylized as it leads step by step to the final appearance of the Red Death. An essay could consider this structure and other features of the tale in relation to the recognizable conventions of popular ghost or horror stories.

5. **Style and diction in "The Masque of the Red Death":** Poe is noted for his dramatic gothic style of writing. Discuss Poe's use of language in this tale.

An essay on this topic should look closely at the language in the story, examining particular examples and mentioning specific techniques such as repetition, alliteration, and rhythm. Also note Poe's genius for creating powerful pictures in his writing, sometimes with just a few words. The writing is designed to frighten the reader; a good essay would therefore point out how Poe's use of language works to shock or unsettle readers.

Compare and Contrast Essays

In planning and writing compare and contrast essays, keep in mind the essential logic of such essays: They both compare and contrast the works they discuss, because similarities and differences provide essential context for each other.

For example, if you compare "The Masque of the Red Death" to a contemporary horror movie, the obvious similarity is that both works are designed to frighten their audiences. The essential contrast, then, might be that they use different methods to achieve the same effect, or it might be that the two works evoke different kinds of fear. Alternatively, you could argue that the two works use similar methods and achieve similar effects. In that case, you would probably point out the way that relatively slight differences serve slightly different ends.

Sample Topics:

1. **Comparing "Masque of the Red Death" to a horror movie:** Stories that frighten us have always been popular. Compare and contrast the methods Poe uses and the effects he achieves in "The Masque of the Red Death" with those of a modern film or films.

   You might begin by identifying what makes Poe's tale frightening: his bizarre settings, striking images, the dark suggestions about Prospero's sanity, and so on. How you relate these devices to those in another work depends on what kind of horror movie you choose for comparison. An essay that pairs Poe's tale with a similarly atmospheric film, such as a tale of the supernatural, might find strong similarities in technique and effect. Where you note differences, you might explain how these differences suit either the somewhat different subject matter in each work or the difference in form between Poe's stylized literary tale and today's theatrical film.

If instead you pair Poe's tale with a film of graphic violence, the contrast in methods would seem paramount. Do the methods work in different ways to create similar effects on the audience? You might argue instead that the effects themselves are different, that Poe's tale and today's slasher movies evoke altogether different species of fear, and explain how each achieves its unique effect.

2. **Comparing Prosperos:** Compare and contrast the character of Prospero in Poe's story to the character of the same name in Shakespeare's play *The Tempest*.

Prospero is the magician in *The Tempest* who makes his home on his own island, apart from human society. On this island, he arranges and controls everything, even the winds themselves. Yet a storm carries to his private sanctuary the very people he left behind. An essay comparing this character to Poe's might note the essential similarities and then explore the associations. Assuming that Poe expected his readers to make connections to Shakespeare's famous play, how do your ideas about that Prospero lend meaning to Poe's tale? Does Poe's story seem in some way to build on, comment on, or perhaps "spin" Shakespeare's tale?

Bibliography for "The Masque of the Red Death"

Bell, H. H., Jr. "'The Masque of the Red Death'—An Interpretation." *South Atlantic Bulletin* 38, no. 4 (1973): 101–04.

Cassuto, Leonard. "The Coy Reaper: Un-masque-ing the Red Death." *Studies in Short Fiction* 25, no. 3 (1988): 317–20.

Chandran, K. Narayana. "Poe's Use of Macbeth in 'The Masque of The Red Death.'" *Papers on Language & Literature* 29, no. 2 (1993): 236.

Cheney, Patrick. "Poe's Use of *The Tempest* and the *Bible* in 'The Masque of the Red Death.'" *English Language Notes* 20, nos. 3–4 (1983): 34.

Dudley, David R. "Dead or Alive: The Booby-Trapped Narrator of Poe's 'The Masque of the Red Death.'" *Studies in Short Fiction* 30, no. 2 (1993): 169–73.

Roppolo, Joseph Patrick. "Meaning and 'The Masque of the Red Death.'" *Tulane Studies in English* 13 (1963): 59–69.

Ruddick, Nicholas. "The Hoax of the Red Death: Poe as Allegorist." *Sphinx* 16, no. 4 (1985): 268–76.

Slick, Richard D. "Poe's 'The Masque of the Red Death.'" *Explicator* 48 (Winter 1989): 24–26.

Thompson, G. R. "Edgar Allan Poe." *Dictionary of Literary Biography.* Vol. 3: *Antebellum Writers in New York and the South.* Ed. Joel Myerson. Detroit: Gale, 1979. 249–97.

Vora, Setu K., and Sundaram V. Ramanan. "Ebola-Poe: A Modern-Day Parallel of the Red Death?" *Emerging Infectious Diseases* 8, no. 12 (2002): 1,521.

"THE PIT AND
THE PENDULUM"

READING TO WRITE

"T HE PIT and the Pendulum" tells a story about the cruel torture and suffering of one man at the hands of the Spanish Inquisition. In the face of harrowing experience and admitted lapses of memory, the narrator attempts to construct a consistent chronology of events, perceptions, and states of mind. The resulting narrative, like many of Poe's tales, lends itself to multiple readings.

In some ways, the story seems to be an adventurous tale of terror, with its succession of exciting escapes from death. In other ways, it appears to be the record of a dream or hallucination, with its fragmentary visual impressions and its references to swooning and dreaming. Along similar lines, the tale might be viewed allegorically or metaphorically, as a depiction of the subconscious mind. At the opposite end of the spectrum, its barely believable succession of mortal dangers and narrow escapes, together with its borrowings from well-known works of Poe's day, might lead some readers to interpret it as a parody.

A number of features complicate the reading of the story, and one of the first jobs of a reader is to sift through the many questions, contradictions, and problems the tale raises. For one thing, the first part of the story, in which the narrator studies his cell and the conditions of his confinement, does not seem to fit with the second part, which is all action and adventure. Nothing seems to come of the extensive examination he makes of the size and shape of his cell. Also odd is the absence of information about the narrator's background. His situation leads the reader inevitably to wonder about its origin. What did he do that got him in trouble? Is he guilty of the crimes with which he is charged? It seems unnatural, somewhat mysterious, that he never even mentions the subject. Still another anomaly is the abrupt ending, in which the narrator is miraculously saved by a character whose existence has never been mentioned. The rescue, as presented, strains belief, and the conclusion in general is one that most readers find dissatisfying.

To see how the story might be read in several different ways, look at the second paragraph of the tale, which comes immediately after the narrator hears his sentence from the judges:

> I had swooned; but still will not say that all of consciousness was lost. What of it there remained I will not attempt to define, or even to describe; yet all was not lost. In the deepest slumber—no! In delirium—no! In a swoon—no! In death—no! even in the grave all is not lost. Else there is no immortality for man. Arousing from the most profound of slumbers, we break the gossamer web of some dream. Yet in a second afterward (so frail may that web have been) we remember not that we have dreamed. In the return to life from the swoon there are two stages: first, that of the sense of mental or spiritual; secondly that of the sense of physical existence. It seems probable that if, upon reaching the second stage, we could recall the impressions of the first, we should find these impressions eloquent in memories of the gulf beyond. And that gulf is—what? How at least shall we distinguish its shadows from those of the tomb? But if the impressions of what I have termed the first stage, are not, at will, recalled, yet, after long interval, do they not come unbidden, while we marvel whence they come? He who has never swooned is not he who finds strange palaces and wildly familiar faces in coals that glow; is not he who beholds floating in mid-air the sad visions that the many may not view; is not he who ponders over the perfume of some novel flower—is not he whose brain grows bewildered with the meaning of some musical cadence which has never before arrested his attention.

Readers expect this paragraph to set the stage for what is to come. What ideas does it offer? For what kind of story does it prepare the reader? It focuses on certain mental states: dreaming, delirium, swooning.

The passage is perplexing at every level. First, while it clearly refers to certain mental states, it is unclear what attitude it means to take toward them. Some of it seems very sensible. Most people have probably experienced upon waking the feeling of recalling a previous consciousness just out of reach but seemingly of profound import. Many would also agree that unconscious thoughts emerge in our lives in fleeting, "unbidden" thoughts and fancies. At other times, however, the text seems to lead into the realm of the paranormal or supernatural, as when it moves from the consciousness of a dream or swoon to consciousness in death.

Readers must try to determine where the narrator stands on the matters he raises. Is he basically normal, or something of a kook? The text gives us hints in both directions, making it difficult or impossible to decide. When he speaks, for example, of the "gulf beyond," it is unclear what he means. Instead of explaining, he poses questions: "And that gulf is—what? How at least shall we distinguish its shadows from those of the tomb?" He further confounds the reader at the end of the paragraph with a string of statements about the man "who has not swooned." The double negatives in these lines seem almost deliberately confusing. Stated in positive terms and simple language, the last sentence states that the type of person who swoons is the type who sees strange figures in fireplace coals, sees visions in midair, and feels suddenly affected by music in ways that surprise even himself. These examples extend the puzzlement by cleverly straddling the line between what is considered normal, if curious, and what is considered bizarre. The narrator is a man who swoons; he has told us that. Does that make him merely someone who, like most people, has imagined pictures in a glowing fire, or is he a crazy man who sees things in midair?

As you think along these lines, what sense does the passage give you about the tale it introduces? If you decide that the man is crazy, you are likely to read his tale as some kind of hallucination or nightmare. Or you might decide that, since he is interested in the nature of these ephemeral mental states, he is creating in his tale a metaphorical picture of what they are like. If you decide that the examples in the paragraph are not really so bizarre, you might read the tale as a basically truthful account of an ordinary man in extraordinary adventures. And again, if you feel that his highly charged language and vague references to things like the "gulf beyond" are just so much mumbo-jumbo, then you will likely treat the story as a kind of joke.

You might also read the tale in terms of the very confusion in the passage. If this segment presents opposing ideas that are difficult to reconcile, could the same be said about the tale as a whole? If the passage leaves the reader with mixed feelings about the narrator and what he is trying to suggest about these paranormal states, is that part of the overall design of the story?

TOPICS AND STRATEGIES
Themes

Just as the tale can be read in different ways, so can a variety of themes be identified. As an adventure, the tale can be read as focusing on the struggle to survive and the mental and emotional equipment humans need to survive. As psychological allegory, the tale seems to focus on the nature of human consciousness, as well as the struggles of the subconscious mind. Religious themes include sin and redemption, death and resurrection.

In writing about any of these themes, try to be metaphorical and allusive rather than literal and reductive. Imagine, for example, writing about the terrors of the prison as representing certain terrors within the human mind. Instead of merely saying that the pit represents the fear of falling, you could explore the implications of falling. When and how do people experience a kind of "falling" in other than the physical sense? Going beyond viewing the pendulum simply as an instrument of death, you might ask what it suggests as an instrument of time. The powerful images that are a hallmark of Poe's work lend themselves to rich discussion.

Sample Topics:

1. **Survival:** How does the story depict the struggle to survive under extreme circumstances? What does it suggest are the keys to survival?

It is extraordinary that the narrator—with his limited resources, hunger, fatigue, disorientation, physical fear, and psychological stress—is able to keep his wits about him, avert the threats he faces, and keep himself alive long enough for help to arrive. What enables him to succeed? An essay might consider his intellectual approach: his persistent effort to understand his circumstances and make rational plans to deal with them. Alternatively, you might focus on the struggle between hope and despair, observing and analyzing the story's repeated references to these competing emotions.

2. **Dreaming:** How might the tale be read as representing dreaming or other dreamlike states?

One approach is to treat the tale itself as the account of a dream. The incidents the narrator describes really happen only in his dream. (It is common in fiction, and perhaps in real life, for people to dream that they have awakened when they have not.) An essay taking this approach would point out the dreamlike features of the tale, including its nightmarish setting, contradictions, arbitrary sequence of events, and more. How might this reading accommodate the abrupt ending of the tale?

An exemplary essay would go beyond showing how the tale resembles a dream. If the tale describes a dream, what ideas about dreaming does it present? Alternatively, an essay might go on to interpret the dream: What does it reveal about the concerns or state of mind of the dreamer?

3. **The subconscious mind:** If the cell is interpreted as representing the human mind, how does the story depict its terrors?

An essay on this topic might first outline reasons for interpreting the story in terms of human consciousness. In making the connection, you might examine the characteristics of the cell: It is dark and confusing; it is fearful, filled with dangers; it is a prison. Consider the cell's most prominent features. What ideas does the pit suggest? What might the pendulum represent? In discussing either or both of these features, you should gather ideas from both the descriptions of the objects themselves and the ways that the narrator responds to them.

4. **Suffering and redemption:** What does the story suggest about human suffering and release from suffering?

You might begin by considering the religious allusions and imagery in the tale. The setting, during the Inquisition, immediately raises religious ideas. The reference to seven candles and seven angels recalls a passage in Revelation (1:12–14), a book of the New Testament that describes a time of great suffering, ending in the final triumph of good over evil. In addition, the narrator's incarceration resembles an entombment, and his miraculous rescue may suggest a resurrection. Numerous connections might be drawn, then, between important religious themes and Poe's story.

Character

The story focuses on a single character but reveals little about him on a personal level. It does not give his name, age, nationality, or religion. The story never explains how he came to be imprisoned, whether justly or unjustly. Why has all this information been withheld?

One answer might be that the character is meant to be viewed not as an individual but rather as a sort of everyman. This is a common strategy in allegory, which focuses on what the character represents. Poe's character can be variously interpreted as representing the human mind or the rational mind or conversely the romantic imagination. An essay on one of these topics would use details about his thoughts and actions to construct a portrait of his mental or emotional makeup.

It is also possible to view the missing information about the character as a deliberate withholding of information on the part of the first-person narrator. Are there other parts of his narrative that suggest that his account is not entirely trustworthy? If so, is he confused, deluded, or deceitful?

Sample Topics:

1. **The narrator as rationalist:** What do the narrator's thoughts and actions reveal about his ability to remain rational under extreme, terrifying circumstances?

   An essay on this topic might examine the narrator's constant attempts to understand what is happening to him, including his thoughts and measurements of the room, which consume much of the tale. You might also discuss the narrator's clever ideas for escaping the dangers to which he is subjected. What enables him to remain so logical under circumstances that would unnerve many?

   The narrator may also display an opposite, irrational side, as discussed below. It is possible to write about either of these two sides or the conflict between them. Does the story depict a character whose mind struggles between rationality and emotionalism?

2. **The narrator as romantic:** Although the narrator thinks carefully about his predicament, he also indulges in dramatic emotionalism. In what ways does he seem romantic or mystical?

   In the passage quoted in the first section of this chapter, the narrator speaks of the man "who does not swoon." From the examples he lists, how would you describe the type of person who swoons? Does the narrator seem to admire this kind of person? Based on his comments and behavior elsewhere in the tale, does the narrator himself resemble such a person?

3. **The unreliable narrator:** How believable is the narrator's version of events? Is there any reason to distrust him?

   Certainly the tale is filled with gaps and contradictions. The narrator offers no information about the crime of which he is accused. He says he does not remember things. He makes careful calculations that later prove false. The events he describes are rather unbelievable, and the ending is almost preposterous. Is the man confused? If so, in what way? Is he deceiving himself, or us, and if so, why? Could he be pulling our leg, or merely entertaining us with a tall tale?

History and Context

The events of the story refer to the Spanish Inquisition, a tribunal started in 1478 that sought to combat religious heresy and became notorious for widespread persecution, torture, and execution. Poe draws upon historical fact as well as actual events that occurred in Toledo, including the capture of that city by French forces at the time of Napoleon Bonaparte.

Between the historical events and Poe's tale, various kinds of connections may be drawn. One strategy is to imagine a story that is similar to "The Pit and the Pendulum" but set in a different time and place. How would this story be different? What ideas present in Poe's tale would be lost? From this exercise you might get a sense of what Poe's historical setting does for the tale.

Sample Topics:

1. **The Inquisition:** In what ways or for what purpose does Poe use the background of the Spanish Inquisition in his tale?

   You might view the tale as a depiction of or commentary on the horrors of the Inquisition. In such a reading, however, the lack of information regarding the narrator's alleged crime and other peculiar features of the tale are difficult to explain. Perhaps more fruitfully, you could consider the Inquisition as an influence on Poe's story. Starting with a viewpoint about the tale and its themes, ask what the Inquisition setting contributes to these ideas. From a psychological point of view, for example, how might the Inquisition serve as a metaphor for human fears or for dark, punishing psychological forces?

2. **Premature burial:** Premature burial was a widespread fear and popular topic in Poe's time. How does this context affect your reading of the tale?

A great deal of research is available on the topic of premature burial, which was one of the leading anxieties of Poe's time. When the prisoner in Poe's story awakens after his swoon, he is consumed by a "fearful idea," which appears to be the fear that he has been buried alive. It may be argued that this fear underlies much of his subsequent behavior. An essay could explore this fear, the nature of the terror, and how it is depicted in the tale.

Alternatively, one might explore Poe's interest in this subject, which was a favorite topic of the media. Magazines were filled with articles on the subject, and Poe himself published a hoax about being buried alive. In "The Pit and the Pendulum," then, was Poe exploiting a topic that he knew attracted readers? Was he satirizing magazine and newspaper stories that he believed did exploit the topic? An essay that provides historical context could be an interesting discussion of Poe's treatment of the subject.

Form and Genre

Writing about form and structure involves exploring how the work is designed. How are the elements of fiction used, and to what effect? Begin with your own response to the story. Are you genuinely swept up in the terrors that beset the prisoner? Or do you find yourself more dispassionately admiring the technique of the story, without being emotionally involved? Some readers may even be amused by the succession of hair-raising dangers and breathtaking escapes. An essay on form and genre could try to point to specific elements in the tale that help account for such reactions. What ingredients make the story seem like a tale of terror? Which might lead you to read it as a parody?

Alternatively, you might take as a starting point some noteworthy feature of the text. The setting, for example, seems in this tale to be more than a mere locale. The ending of the story seems peculiarly abrupt. You could identify some such feature and discuss its effect within the work as a whole.

Sample Topics:

1. **Setting:** Analyze Poe's use of the prison cell as part of the overall design of the story.

A paper on this topic could take many directions, and you might begin by considering all the ways the prison cell functions in the tale. You could explore how Poe's descriptions of the cell help create the terrifying atmosphere of the tale. Reading allegorically or metaphorically, consider what the features of the cell might represent. The prison is also an object of study by the narrator: His contradictory observations regarding the cell contribute greatly to the ambiguity and puzzlement that characterize the story. Finally, with its pit and pendulum and collapsing walls all threatening death, the cell is an actual agent, if not a character, in the story.

2. **Sensation story:** In what ways does the story depict human emotions and/or play upon the emotions of its readers?

Although it is commonly believed that Poe was personally drawn to the tale of terror, in fact such tales were widely published and read in Poe's time. These are often called tales of sensation because of their strong focus on the sensations their characters experience. An essay could list and discuss the typical ingredients of the tale of sensation and specifically identify the devices Poe uses in his tale. You might consider, too, the appeal of such stories, including some of the deep human fears that Poe's story activates: the fear of falling, enclosure, evisceration, and so forth.

You might also consider the capacity of this genre to exploit the public's appetite for sensation. Where and how can you draw the line between earnest treatments of human emotion and exploitative sensationalism? Ask yourself whether "The Pit and the Pendulum" is exploitative and what basis you can use for answering that question.

3. **Parody:** In a magazine article titled "How to Write a Blackwood Article," Poe parodied "tales of terror, taste . . . sensation." Should "The Pit and the Pendulum" be read as a parody of this kind of tale?

An essay on this topic would weigh the sensational elements of the story in terms of their effects on the reader and the literary context of Poe's time. Are these elements genuinely frightening or so exaggerated that they cannot be taken seriously? Other factors should also be considered. Poe lifted several prominent story elements, such as the compressing walls, from earlier stories. (A discussion of these elements and their sources can be found in Bruce Weiner's article "Poe and Blackwood's Tale of Sensation," in *Poe and His Times: The Artist and His Milieu,* pp. 45–65.) An essay could consider whether these borrowings suggest parody. You might also consider the abrupt ending of the story, which some readers find so miraculous as to be silly.

An essay could adopt either position on the question; it should at least acknowledge reasons on both sides of the issue.

4. **Anomalies:** Do some features of the tale seem to violate basic rules or conventions of storytelling? How do you account for these apparent lapses?

One problem for some readers is that the narrator's long consideration of the size and shape of the room seems unrelated to later events. Another is that the story seems to jump from one danger to another rather than progressing in some order. A third problem is the happy ending that seems to come out of nowhere. In discussing any of these problems, it would be best not to dismiss the feature as a weakness in the tale but rather to develop a theory about how this feature fits the design of the story. You might argue, for example, that the narrator's ruminations about the size of the room represent his attempt to remain rational, and the fact that the ruminations come to nothing shows the uselessness of rationality in the face of real terror.

Compare and Contrast Essays

Viewed as a tale of terror, "The Pit and the Pendulum" invites comparison with other horror stories. You might compare this tale to another Poe story, another short story by one of Poe's contemporaries, or a more modern tale. Whatever your choice, the key challenge is to develop a thesis about the two works. Is there a pattern to the similarities? What is the effect of the differences? The answers to questions like these can provide good thesis statements, points around which meaningful essays may be built.

Sample Topics:

1. **Comparing tales of terror:** Compare "The Pit and the Pendulum" to another tale of terror.

   You might compare the tale to another Poe story, such as "MS. Found in a Bottle" or "A Descent into the Maelstrom." Or you might choose a story from Poe's time by another author, perhaps considering one of Poe's source stories, "The Iron Shroud" by William Mudford or "The Man in the Bell" by William Maginn. After noting similarities between the stories, discuss the differences. How do the tales treat their subjects differently? How do these differences reflect different aims? What does the different execution say about the different craft or methods of the authors?

2. **Comparing "The Pit and the Pendulum" to "A Predicament":** In 1838 Poe published a parody of the popular tale of terror in a piece called "A Predicament." How does this spoof compare to "The Pit and the Pendulum"?

   "A Predicament," a tale-within-a-tale that appears in an article variously titled "The Psyche Zenobia" and "How to Write a Blackwood Article," describes a close brush with horrible death and an amazing escape. What happens if you put this comic tale side by side with "The Pit and the Pendulum"? You might be struck by the similarities and argue that Poe's Inquisition story, though it pretends to be serious, in fact employs the same methods as the ridiculous "Predicament." Alternatively, you might examine how the two works differ, explaining specifically what makes one tale serious and the other humorous.

Bibliography for "The Pit and the Pendulum"

Bondensen, Jan. *Buried Alive: The Terrifying History of Our Most Primal Fear.* New York: W. W. Norton & Co., 2001.

Burduck, Michael L. *Grim Phantasms: Fear in Poe's Short Fiction.* New York: Garland Publishing, 1992.

Engel, Leonard W. "Psychological Crisis and Enclosure in Edgar Allan Poe's 'The Pit and the Pendulum.'" *CEA Critic* 45 (March and May 1983): 28–31.

Goddu, Teresa A. "Poe, Sensationalism, and Slavery." *The Cambridge Companion to Edgar Allan Poe.* Ed. Kevin J. Hayes. Cambridge: Cambridge UP, 2002. 92–132.

Ketterer, David. *The Rationale of Deception in Poe.* Baton Rouge: Louisiana State UP, 1979.

Lawes, Rochies. "The Dimensions of Terror: Mathematical Imagery in 'The Pit and the Pendulum.'" *Poe Studies* 16 (June 1983): 5–7.

Weiner, Bruce I. "Poe and the Blackwood's Tale of Sensation." *Poe and His Times: The Artist and His Milieu.* Ed. Benjamin Franklin Fisher IV. Baltimore: Edgar Allan Poe Society, 1990. 45–65.

"THE GOLD-BUG"

READING TO WRITE

"T HE GOLD-BUG" offers an exciting treasure hunt that grows more interesting and puzzling the more the reader ponders it. It is a story of buried pirate treasure, of wealth and of humans' attempts to acquire and keep it. It is a story about madness or apparent madness or feigned madness. It certainly is a story about misleading appearances, as suggested by Legrand's supposed madness and also Captain Kidd's treasure map, which at first appears to be a worthless scrap of paper. The second half of the tale seems almost a how-to article on cryptography. A tale of puzzles and detection, the story itself is a puzzle, which readers must unravel just as Legrand unlocks the secret of Kidd's treasure.

One source of the confusion is the narrator. The story is told by Legrand's friend, who was involved in much of the action and, at the time he writes the story, knows the truth of the matter. Yet instead of giving an accurate account of what went on, he reveals only what he believed at the time. This gives a distorted view of Legrand and his actions that only later is corrected. As a result of this narrative framework, it is difficult to know what to believe—about Legrand, about the narrator, and about the aims of the story. The reader must piece together the evidence of the text to uncover its hidden meanings.

To observe the complexities of interpretation, look at the part of the tale just prior to the discovery of the treasure, before anyone can be sure that there is in fact a treasure to be found. The narrator writes:

Could I have depended, indeed, upon Jupiter's aid, I would have had no hesitation in attempting to get the lunatic home by force; but I was too well assured of the old negro's disposition, to hope that he would assist me, under any circumstances, in a personal contest with his master. I made no doubt that the latter had been infected with some of the innumerable Southern superstitions about money buried, and that his phantasy had received confirmation by the finding of the *scarabaeus*, or, perhaps, by Jupiter's obstinacy in maintaining it to be "a bug of real gold." A mind disposed to lunacy would readily be led away by such suggestions—especially if chiming in with favorite preconceived ideas—and then I called to mind the poor fellow's speech about the beetle's being "the index of his fortune." Upon the whole, I was sadly vexed and puzzled, but, at length, I concluded to make a virtue of necessity—to dig with a good will, and thus the sooner to convince the visionary, by ocular demonstration, of the fallacy of the opinions he entertained.

If these words are taken at face value, the narrator leaves no doubt that Legrand is insane. Yet if the passage is considered in relation to the story as a whole, the narrator's remarks take on a totally different meaning, since he subsequently reveals that Legrand knows exactly what he is doing. In context, therefore, the passage raises a series of cascading questions.

At the level of character, one question is how the narrator could have been so certain about Legrand—and so wrong. Is there something about the narrator that blinds him to the truth? Was he in fact less certain than he claims? If so, why might he dissemble on the matter? At the end of the story Legrand says that he deliberately encouraged the narrator in his mistaken belief. How great a factor was Legrand's ruse?

In terms of theme, the tale raises questions about rationality and madness. In the quoted passage, the narrator presents himself as the voice of reason, yet subsequent events will reveal Legrand as the man with the astute and logical mind. This reversal suggests as a further theme the conflict between appearance and reality. This theme is figured by the secret map, which appears at first to be a scrap of worthless paper.

You might also address questions in relation to the story as a work of art that is designed in a particular way and has certain effects on its readers. The tale creates an anomalous situation in which the narrator focuses on something that proves to be incorrect. What effect does this peculiar structure achieve? Does the story truly mislead you into believing the narrator when he says that Legrand is mad? If so, what purpose or effect does this trickery serve? Or do you not fully accept the narrator's conclusion about Legrand? In that case, does the story mean to raise in readers' minds the question whether Legrand is mad? Again, why? Or does the story really mean to focus the reader's thoughts on the narrator himself and the disparity between his conclusions and the reader's own?

This last idea, when considered closely, is curious indeed: How can it be that while you rely on the narrator for all your information, you nevertheless arrive at ideas quite different from his? This avenue of thought leads to yet another approach, in which you would view the story as dealing with the subject of reading itself. "The Gold-Bug" details the process by which a man discerns hidden meaning in a written text. But this is very much what you do when in reading the tale. You not only consider what it says but also try to fit together sometimes confusing or seemingly contradictory pieces in order to discover what you take to be its meaning. This tale, more than some, also forces you to reflect on your own process. Tracing your thoughts about the structure of the story leads you to consider not only what the story is saying but how you decide what it is saying.

TOPICS AND STRATEGIES
Themes

"The Gold-Bug" involves the discovery of great wealth, the suggestion of madness, the deciphering of secret writing, and more. The tale also features a succession of striking images: objects such as pirate treasure, a gold beetle, a skull, a coded message, and disappearing ink. Through such images, the story suggests ideas that it does not come right out and say. Therefore, a good starting point in thinking about themes in the tale is a consideration of these richly suggestive images. What ideas might you draw, for example, from connecting the images of wealth with the images of death? What ideas surround buried treasure, disappearing ink, and coded messages, and how might these ideas be applied to the people in the tale and their actions?

Sample Topics:

1. **Wealth:** What ideas does the tale suggest about wealth and the role it plays in human society?

   A tale about buried treasure obviously raises the issue of money. An essay on this topic might explore the lure of wealth in terms of Legrand's seemingly manic behavior at the prospect of finding a treasure, Captain Kidd's own extreme precautions for keeping his hiding place secret, and the references to the many people who searched for Kidd's treasure. Is Jupiter right when he says that the "gold bug" bites everyone it comes near? What is it like to be bitten by this bug? You might also consider Legrand's status as a former aristocrat who has lost his wealth and the "mortification" this causes him.

2. **Mystification:** Like Captain Kidd's treasure and his written directions for finding it, Legrand's true state of mind is hidden from Jupiter and the narrator. Discuss the ideas of secrecy and obfuscation in the tale.

   The divergence between appearance and reality is a major theme in many works of literature. In most works, however, the characters' misreading of reality is the result of some kind of blindness or flaw in themselves. Such a viewpoint might be applied to "The Gold-Bug," but here much of the confusion seems instead the result of deliberate design. Kidd deliberately used disappearing ink and cipher, because he did not want his treasure to be found. Legrand's behavior is more peculiar. Though perfectly sane, he encourages the narrator's belief that he is mad. Legrand's purpose, he says, is to "punish" his friend. What role does Legrand's obfuscation or hoaxing play in the story? What is his motivation, and what is the effect on the narrator and the reader?

3. **Death/rebirth:** Legrand's discovery of Kidd's treasure does not make him newly wealthy but restores him to a life he had lost. How do objects and events in the tale foster ideas of death and rebirth, and what ideas do they suggest about human renewal?

Examine the story closely for images and suggestions of death and rebirth appear throughout the tale. Examples include the *Jolly Roger* and the skull in the tree, the scythe and spade, the buried treasure, and the invisible writing that reappears when placed near the fire. The gold bug itself, which is frequently referred to as a *scarabaeus,* points to the ancient Egyptians' symbol of rebirth. What ideas does the interplay of these images provide about the process of renewal: how it happens, what it requires, or what it feels like?

4. **Luck and fate:** Legrand points out to the narrator the extraordinary succession of accidents that were necessary for the treasure map to come to light. Is Legrand the beneficiary of mere coincidence, or is some special force at work?

You might adopt any opinion on this question, but the ideas you present should say something meaningful about the tale. Are there indications that Legrand himself believes that his good fortune is more than a matter of accident? If so, does that tell you what kind of person Legrand is, does it tell you how people typically think about their lives, or does the tale itself seem to agree that human lives are ruled by fate? Conversely, if you argue that Legrand's discovery is purely the product of coincidence, does the tale thereby imply that the most important things in life are purely a matter of chance? You might also argue that the tale means to raise these questions without giving them a definitive answer.

Other approaches are also possible. You might argue that while luck put the map in Legrand's hands, his retrieval of the treasure was due to his perspicacity in recognizing that the map was more than just a dirty piece of paper and his ingenuity and determination in deciphering the message. Or you might consider the matter of coincidence in terms of the nature of literature. Does the act of reading a story involve at its essence the attempt to make sense of events? Do readers not assume that the events in a story are somehow connected—that they must add up to something meaningful? If this is so, does that make a story of total coincidence a logical impossibility?

5. **Reading:** The tale devotes considerable time to Legrand's explanation of how he was able to read and understand the cipher. In what ways can the tale be read as an analysis of the process of reading itself?

Consider Legrand's procedures. First, he says, one must already know the language in which the message was written. After identifying the words comes the process of deciding what they refer to, in order to make sense of them. How well do these actions represent what people do when they read—how they attempt to make sense out of a story? What specific comments does Legrand make that shed light on what readers do? What skills, behavior, and assumptions does Legrand bring to the task? How, for example, is he able to make sense out of the peculiar references in the message?

Character

A good starting point for writing about character is to choose one person and one point of interest about him or her. In the case of William Legrand, many ideas spring to mind: his loss of wealth and self-imposed exile from society, his apparent madness, his mental acumen in discovering and deciphering the secret message. An essay on character might start by identifying a particular aspect of the character's makeup and pointing out specific parts of the text that reveal this trait. An exemplary essay would go further, considering how this trait complements, or contrasts with, another of the character's traits; how the character is similar to or contrasts with another character; or how the trait is related to the theme of the story.

Sample Topics:

1. **Legrand's rationalism:** What do Legrand's methods in solving
   the mystery of the treasure show about his personality?

   An essay on this topic might examine the methodical process by which Legrand decodes and interprets Captain Kidd's
   cipher. It might also consider the sometimes intuitive reasoning that leads to his discovery of the secret writing. What can
   you infer from his belief that any mystery that a human being
   can devise can be solved?

   Other facts may be seen as either complementing or con-
   tradicting the image of Legrand as a rationalist. What inferences can you draw, for example, from his "presentiment" of
   good fortune or his desire to punish the narrator for thinking
   him mad? What personal qualities apart from intellect enable
   him to succeed when others would give up the problem as
   hopeless?

2. **The narrator's blindness:** On the night that the treasure is discovered, the narrator is completely mistaken about the nature of
   events. What is it about him that keeps him from seeing events
   as they are?

   It may be useful for you to compare your own reactions to
   Legrand's behavior with those of the narrator. Do you believe
   Legrand's behavior to be senseless, as the narrator does? Or
   do you assume that it somehow makes sense, even if you cannot guess how? You might also wonder how the narrator can
   so badly misread a man who is supposed to be a close friend.
   Indeed, Legrand himself expresses annoyance with the narrator for this very reason.

3. **Jupiter:** What do Jupiter's words and actions suggest about his
   attitudes and values?

   One approach to this topic would be to consider the numerous
   indications of Jupiter's personal devotion to Legrand. You might

also reflect on the opinions Jupiter expresses—which, while lacking the intellectual insight of Legrand, reflect an intuitive grasp of the truth. Although he seems ignorant in believing that the beetle is made of gold, on a metaphorical level he is right. Similarly, when he speaks of the gold bug biting everyone who comes near it, he is actually making a profound observation. An exceptional essay might combine the two aspects of Jupiter's character: To him, the pursuit of wealth is madness; service to another human is what life is about.

History and Context

Captain Kidd was a real pirate, executed in England in 1701. He did sail the east coast of the United States, and he did bury treasure. One trove was found on Gardiner's Island during his lifetime. It was widely believed, and by some people still is, that more treasure is hidden elsewhere. An essay could present research on the historical Kidd and draw connections to aspects of Poe's story.

Kidd and his treasure have also found their way into story and song, and you might choose to explore the legendary pirate. How does Captain Kidd figure in the popular imagination, and what implications does this have for your reading of Poe's tale?

Either of these approaches might also be adopted with regard to the tale's allusions to things Egyptian. The hieroglyphics and the *scarabaeus* are references to aspects of Egyptian culture. They also suggest popular perceptions of Egypt as mysterious and exotic. Starting in the 1820s with the deciphering of the Rosetta stone, America was swept up in an Egypt fad that pervaded aspects of culture from architecture and home decoration to the mummy displays by the showman P. T. Barnum.

Sample Topics:

1. **Egyptology:** Ancient Egypt was a subject of great interest in Poe's time. How are Egyptian beliefs and iconography used in this tale?

   The most important image is the gold bug itself, which the narrator repeatedly refers to as a *scarabaeus,* the sacred dung beetle of ancient Egypt. An essay could present research on the scarab beetle and its use and meaning in Egyptian religion and relate these findings to the images and themes of death and rebirth in Poe's tale.

2. **Captain Kidd:** Though not an actual participant in the action, Captain Kidd is an essential presence in the story. How does the history of Captain Kidd affect your reading of the tale?

Kidd's story may be viewed as adding a feeling of adventure and romance to the tale, or a feeling of horror. Kidd's history may also add layers of significance to the treasure itself. What meaning might attach, for example, to the manner in which Kidd accumulated this wealth and the deadly lengths he went to in order to keep secret its whereabouts? You might also explore the legendary status of Captain Kidd and the persistent searches for his treasure. What does his popularity add to the ideas in the story?

Form and Genre

Considering the form and structure of "The Gold-Bug" is essential in deciding what the tale is really about. The search for buried treasure might incline you to classify the story as an adventure. The adventure, however, is over about halfway through the tale. Moreover, if the story is about an exciting hunt for buried treasure, why does it not say this and let the reader participate in the quest to find the hidden writing, decipher the message, search out the hiding place, and finally uncover the treasure?

Instead, most readers experience the adventurous part of the tale less as an adventure than a puzzle. Some may suspect that Legrand is not mad, as the narrator believes, and may try to guess what Legrand's true purpose is. Others may confidently conclude that he is searching for treasure and wonder why his close friend cannot see the same. In either case, the story has moved the focus to something different from adventure. An essay could describe the reader's reactions and the passages that give rise to these reactions. Next it should propose an explanation or theory: What effect does the story have—what does it achieve—by producing these reactions in the reader?

Sample Topics:

1. **The two-part story:** The first half of the story describes the search for and discovery of the treasure. The second half details the process that enabled Legrand to solve the mystery of Captain Kidd's secret message. Explain how this structure affects your reading of the tale.

As suggested above, as the structure of the tale shifts the focus away from traditional adventure, it raises other issues. An essay could deal with any one of these issues—or more than one if they seem to fit together. The first half of the tale focuses on the narrator's belief that Legrand is mad. You might consider why the narrator is so mistaken or, from a different point of view, why the story makes so much of this issue in the first half and drops the idea—or seems to drop it—in the second.

In the second half, why does the tale explain Legrand's methods at such exhaustive length? This section reveals a good deal about cryptography, but what does it add to the story up to this point?

How are the two halves of the story connected? In the first half Legrand is believed to be mad; in the second he appears to be very clever. Is the story suggesting that genius is often mistaken for madness? Or that Legrand's cleverness is just another form of the frenzy described in him before? Also note that the tale reflects the mind-set of its narrator. At first he was certain that Legrand was mad, but now that the money has been found, he entertains no such doubts. Might the tale be commenting on how attitudes toward a person's sanity or intelligence depend on his or her material success?

You might take a completely different approach if, as suggested elsewhere in this chapter, you view Legrand's deciphering of the message as a kind of metaphor for reading. In this case, you might view the first half of the tale as an illustration of the second. What is wrong with the narrator's "reading" of the situation? Why do readers comprehend events more accurately (assuming that they do)?

2. **The setting of the tale:** "The Gold-Bug" is somewhat unusual among Poe's tales in that it is set in a specific, actual locale. How do the realistic details of the setting affect your experience of the story?

It is easy to argue that the realistic details make the story more credible and thus more exciting. Do the details also make the social setting more immediate? Does this help foreground the social issues that the story raises?

Captain Kidd was a real figure, and at the same time a legendary one. Similarly, accounts of searches for his buried treasure were both factual and the stuff of popular fiction. To some readers, Poe's tale itself seems poised between the realistic and the fanciful. An essay could examine this idea and explain how the naturalistic details in the story operate in counterpoint to elements of plot and character that seem quite conventional and contrived.

Compare and Contrast Essays

To write an essay of this kind, you must first find some point of comparison, either between elements in a single tale or between corresponding elements in different tales. Some similarity must exist for comparison to be meaningful. The relative degree of similarity and difference that you discuss depends on what you are comparing and what you discover of interest. If you compare Legrand to the narrator, for instance, you might focus on the qualities that enable him to see and understand what the narrator cannot. If you compare Legrand to Poe's detective Auguste Dupin, you might focus more on the similarities in their approaches despite their addressing quite different problems.

Sample Topics:

1. **Comparing the characters' "sight":** "The Gold-Bug" can be viewed in terms of what the characters can and cannot see. Compare and contrast any two characters, or all three, in relation to what each is able to understand.

In one sense, Legrand sees the most. He is the only one who sees the scrap of paper for what it is and is able to unravel its secret. Jupiter, however, as discussed in the section on character, shows a different kind of insight, which both Legrand and the narrator lack. An essay could compare Legrand's methodical understanding with Jupiter's insight. Or it might compare Jupiter with the narrator. Both men believe that Legrand is mad, yet they differ on numerous issues, such as Jupiter's intention to beat Legrand, the narrator's desire to take Legrand home by force, and the two men's varying levels of cooperation in the treasure hunt itself.

2. **Comparing "The Gold-Bug" to "The Purloined Letter":** These two tales bear striking resemblances to each other. Compare the structure, character, and/or themes of these tales.

An essay could discuss any of several points of similarity. Structurally, both tales revolve around puzzles that are presented and solved in the first half and explained at length in the second. Thematically, both tales concern themselves with issues about things seen and hidden and about the mental process by which what is hidden is revealed. The characters Dupin and Legrand are remarkably similar, from their exceptional analytical abilities to their capacity for personal vindictiveness.

Bibliography for "The Gold Bug"

Clifford, Barry, and Paul Perry. *Return to Treasure Island and the Search for Captain Kidd*. New York: Harper Paperbacks, 2004.

Cordingly, David. *Pirates: Terror on the High Seas from the Caribbean to the South China Sea*. North Dighton, MA: World Publications, 1999.

Dilalla Toner, Jennifer. "The 'Remarkable Effect' of 'Silly Words': Dialect and Signature in 'The Gold Bug.'" *Arizona Quarterly* 49 (Spring 1993): 1–20.

Hennely, Mark M., Jr. "Le Grand Captain Kidder and His Bogus Bug." *Studies in Short Fiction* 17 (Winter 1980): 77–79.

Hoffman, Daniel. "Disentanglements." *Poe Poe Poe Poe Poe Poe Poe*. New York: Doubleday, 1972. 125–33.

Matthews, James W. "Legrand's Golden Vision: Meaning in 'The Gold Bug.'" *CEA* 53 (Spring–Summer 1991): 23–29.

Phillips, Elizabeth C. "'His Right of Attendance': The Image of the Black Man in the Works of Poe and Two of His Contemporaries." *No Fairer Land: Studies in Southern Literature before 1900.* Ed. J. Lasley Dameron and James W. Matthews. Troy, NY: Whitson, 1986. 172–84.

St. Armand, Barton Levi. "Poe's 'sober Mystification': The Uses of Alchemy in 'The Gold Bug.'" *Poe Studies* 4 (1971): 1–7.

Shell, Marc. "The Gold Bug." *Genre* 13 (Spring 1980): 11–30.

Zachs, Richard. *The Pirate Hunter: The True Story of Captain Kidd.* New York: Hyperion Books, 2002.

"THE BLACK CAT"

READING TO WRITE

INTERPRETING "THE Black Cat" is a challenge in the literal sense, in that the narrator begins his tale by defying the reader to figure it out:

> Hereafter, perhaps, some intellect may be found which will reduce my phantasm to the common-place—some intellect more calm, more logical, and far less excitable than my own, which will perceive, in the circumstances I detail with awe, nothing more than an ordinary succession of very natural causes and effects.

The narrator proceeds to describe a series of events that does indeed defy belief. He says that he killed his cat. That night, his house burned down, and the only wall left standing contained the image of the cat. Soon a second, virtually identical cat appeared, apparently out of nowhere. Driven to frenzy by the cat, and following an attempt to kill it, the man now killed his wife. He safely hid her body in a wall in his cellar, but the cat, walled up with her, shrieked and alerted the police to the hiding place.

Three general approaches suggest themselves as ways to make sense of this extraordinary tale:

1. Supernatural: If the cat is a ghost (or a witch, as the narrator's wife suggests) that has come back from death to avenge its killing, then any and all events are possible. The task of interpretation becomes mainly metaphorical: What figurative meanings do the cat's actions suggest? This is a viable approach; its greatest

weakness is the generally naturalistic tone and setting of the tale, along with the narrator's introductory suggestion that beneath its extraordinary surface the tale in fact makes sense.

2. Psychological: Overcome by alcohol abuse and by guilt, the narrator could be imagining things. This approach fits the naturalistic tone of the tale and its prominent psychological overtones. The narrator is not imagining everything, however. The house really does burn down, something does appear on his bedroom wall, and a second cat does appear, for these events are witnessed by others. Interpretation involves deciding which events are actual occurrences, perhaps brought on by psychological forces, and which can be ascribed to an overactive imagination.

3. Skeptical: If in real life a man, convicted of murdering his wife, told the fantastic tale our narrator offers, you would instantly conclude that he was lying. If you read the tale from this viewpoint, you might cast a cold eye on the narrator's expressions of terror and remorse. You would assume that his wife was the intended victim all along and would search his testimony for weak points, implausible explanations, and internal contradictions. You are likely to doubt that a second identical cat could have appeared out of nowhere or that the figure of the dead cat appeared on the bedroom wall. More likely, there was only one cat: It was not Pluto whose figure protruded from the bedroom wall; it was the wife's. Such a reading may make sense of otherwise inexplicable parts of the story, if sufficient textual support can be found.

Examining one passage in the story will show how it might be used to support these different avenues of interpretation. The following passage describes the appearance of the "second" cat:

One night as I sat, half stupefied, in a den of more than infamy, my attention was suddenly drawn to some black object, reposing upon the head of one of the immense hogsheads of Gin, or of Rum, which constituted the chief furniture of the apartment. I had been looking steadily at the top of this hogshead for some minutes, and what now caused me surprise was the fact that I had not sooner perceived the object thereupon. I approached it, and touched it with my hand. It was a black cat—a very large one—fully as large as Pluto, and closely resembling him in every respect but one. Pluto had not a white hair upon any portion of his body; but this cat had a large, although indefinite splotch of white, covering nearly the whole region of the breast.

Upon my touching him, he immediately arose, purred loudly, rubbed against my hand, and appeared delighted with my notice. This, then, was the very creature of which I was in search. I at once offered to purchase it of the landlord; but this person made no claim to it—knew nothing of it—had never seen it before.

What stands out most in the passage is the manner in which the cat appears, which is in every way marvelous. How can a man look steadily at something for minutes and then suddenly see a cat there?

The seemingly magical appearance, along with the reaction of the landlord, suggests that the cat is something other than an ordinary creature. Considering the strange apparition on the bedroom wall and the wife's comment that all black cats are witches, it is natural to view the cat as supernatural. Yet the passage simultaneously suggests other avenues of interpretation. The cat could be a figment of the man's imagination. He says that he was searching for such a cat, and now it appears to his eye where nothing had been before. What psychological need does the cat fill? Is the man, burdened by guilt, seeking to bring his cat back to life in order to undo his killing of it? Or since the cat will prove to be the instrument of discovery and punishment, does the man's wish for a new cat suggest that a part of him seeks the punishment that the cat will bring about?

Also note the appearance of the cat at a time when the narrator is "half stupefied" in a tavern, a point that raises anew the issue of his alcoholism, which he has blamed for his violent character. The appearance of the cat in this setting connects the agent of the man's destruction with his alcohol abuse, supporting a reading of the story as a tale about the evils of alcohol.

At the same time, the passage also invites a reading of the story as a deliberate attempt by a premeditated murderer to deceive. The narrator has told us that his story has a logical explanation, and in real life cats do not appear out of nowhere. The man must be lying, it seems, but what is the truth? If this is not a magical new cat, it could be the same cat. But if that is true, since we do not believe in ghosts, the man's claim that he killed the cat is false. What, then, did he really do when he says he killed his cat? Study the rest of the story for further clues.

The diversity of possible readings is a prominent feature of the tale that is well worth considering. Some readers, however, find such ambiguity bewildering, if not irritating. It is not necessary for an essay to address a broad range of interpretations. You might instead choose a single aspect of the tale that speaks to you and explore that idea in depth.

TOPICS AND STRATEGIES
Themes

The narrator kills his wife, is apprehended, and faces execution. That much is clear. The forces that bring this to pass, however, are not so clear. You may doubt whether the man's alcohol abuse can really have effected a complete change in his character. You may question his true motive in killing his wife. And you may struggle to decide what ultimately brings the man to justice. Is it a cat with supernatural abilities or the workings of his own conscience? The ambiguities in the tale thus elicit ruminations upon a range of themes while supporting a variety of interpretations.

Sample Topics:

1. **The moral order:** When people say that crime does not pay or that murder will out, they are expressing a belief that moral forces exist in the world that tend to bring evil to light and exact punishment. How does "The Black Cat" support such a concept?

   An essay on this topic would explain how the agency of the seemingly supernatural cat works to expose and punish the narrator. You might mention the fire that occurs the same day that the cat is hanged, the mysterious appearance of the cat's figure on the bedroom wall, and the final exposure of the wife's body by the scream of the cat. A reading along these lines could also consider the reactions of the narrator. Does his bewilderment at what has happened suggest a failure to recognize the moral order of the universe?

2. **Conscience and parapraxis:** What does the story suggest about the workings of the human conscience?

If the cat is thought of as representing the narrator's conscience, then the agency of his punishment is actually within his own mind. To write on this topic, you might consider how the behavior of the man toward his cat mirrors that of a man trying to escape a guilty conscience. Observe, however, that the man's reactions are ambivalent, for after the death of Pluto, he actively searches for a new cat.

Does any of his other behavior support the theory that as much as he seeks to avoid exposure and punishment, another part of him actively invites it? The term *parapraxis* is applied to errors that are believed to arise from and reveal a person's unconscious motives. The narrator's most glaring blunder is to rap with his stick on the wall that hides his wife's body. He says that he does this in order to assure the police of his innocence. But the effect is to bring his downfall. Could sealing up the cat in the wall reflect a similar unconscious design? What other psychological motivation is suggested by walling up the cat? Might a similar force be at work when he burns down his house the day that he hangs his cat?

You might even consider the man's story itself. Is there evidence in it that he is trying to hide the true depth of his guilt? If so, do lapses in his story help bring the truth to light?

3. **Perversity:** The narrator gives perversity as the reason that he kills his cat. Discuss the theme of perversity and its role in the tale.

The narrator defines *perverseness* as a primal impulse in human beings to commit actions precisely because they know they should not. Is this an important force in human life, and how well does it explain the narrator's behavior? In terms of the story, what gives rise to this impulse, and where does it lead? If it is perversity that leads the narrator to kill Pluto—an evil deed—is it also a form of perversity that leads him to rap on the cellar wall, ultimately bringing his own punishment?

Alternatively, might perversity be an intellectual scapegoat, something we blame for behavior whose true source we wish to conceal? On one page the narrator blames the "Fiend Intemperance" for his abuse of his wife. On the next he blames "Perverseness" for hanging his cat. Does perversity help you understand the man or inhibit your understanding?

4. **Spouse abuse:** How does the story treat the topic of wife abuse?

The narrator admits to physically abusing his wife, although he speaks less on the subject than he does about his treatment of his cat. Is this because his treatment of his wife is too painful to face? Is it possible that he has substituted his cat for his wife? His behavior toward Pluto seems to follow a cycle that is common in spouse abuse: abuse followed by remorse and self-recrimination, which turns into a redoubled animosity toward the object of the abuse.

You might also explore the causes of the man's behavior. The narrator says that when he was young his friends made fun of his docility and tenderness of heart. Did feelings of weakness contribute to his later brutality? He says that alcohol abuse changed his personality. Readers may conclude that his drinking did indeed lead to bouts of abusive behavior—a common occurrence—without accepting his alcoholism as the entire cause of his violence toward his wife.

Character

Theme and character in "The Black Cat" are closely linked, for what the story is about revolves largely around the force or forces that drive the main character. Essays on either theme or character would include a discussion of his relevant behavior and its implications. An essay on character would tend to focus more within the story, explaining, for example, how conscience controls this man and, perhaps, what has brought him to this state. An essay on theme would tend to emphasize the ideas or feelings the story generates about the role of conscience in human behavior. These distinctions, however, are by no means absolute.

Sample Topics:

1. **The narrator and his conscience:** How does the story show the narrator as a man struggling with his own conscience?

   Ideas to consider here are similar to those discussed in the section on themes. The narrator expresses guilt and remorse about his behavior. The cat seems to embody these feelings, so his behavior toward the cat may be viewed as representing his feelings toward a punishing conscience. An essay could discuss his specific actions toward the cat and how they demonstrate an attempt to escape from it. You might also examine how his description of events sometimes seems aimed at rationalizing his guilt, as discussed below.

   These acts suggest an impulse to escape, but an essay might argue that the man vacillates between accepting and evading guilt. How do you interpret his stated desire to find a replacement for Pluto and his almost seeming to will the new cat into existence? You might comment, too, on the final exposure of his crime. Although the cat shrieks, it is the man himself who precipitates the scream by tapping on the wall.

2. **The narrator's rationalization:** In what ways does the narrator avoid accepting responsibility for what he has done?

   Although he admits to wrongdoing, in several respects he does not seem to assume full responsibility for his behavior. In his opening remarks, as well as others, he casts himself as a victim. He blames his abuse of his wife on "the Fiend Intemperance" and his killing of his cat on a phenomenon he calls "Perverseness."

To what extent do these seem more like excuses for his behavior than genuine explanations?

You might also consider the offhand way he speaks about his abuse and killing of his wife. In contrast, he describes his assault on his cat far more graphically and his killing of it with almost inordinate remorse. Why are his emotions so misplaced? Is his psyche able to bear the lesser guilt but not the greater?

3. **The narrator's alcoholism:** The narrator says that alcohol abuse changed him from an unusually kind and tender man to a wife beater and murderer. Discuss the role of alcohol in the man's behavior.

The narrator's claim raises many questions. If you accept that alcohol changed the man, you may still inquire into this process. Did the alcohol bring out latent impulses? Was his former loving disposition an attempt to mask or suppress more aggressive feelings? And, taking this idea a step further, can you consider his descent into alcoholism a psychological strategy to liberate those deep and impermissible impulses? Alternatively, did his alcoholism give birth to altogether new hateful feelings? The text gives no suggestion that his wife made recriminations about his drinking. It says instead that he "grew more moody, more irritable, more regardless of the feelings of others." It is possible to speculate that the narrator's alcoholism engendered feelings of guilt or self-loathing that he turned outward toward those around him. Readers must decide for themselves whether the text gives sufficient grounds for such a speculation.

Yet another approach, suggested under the previous topic, is to view the alcoholism as a psychological scapegoat, an attempt to evade responsibility for his behavior.

4. **The narrator as premeditated murderer:** Since the narrator is about to be executed, it can be inferred that a jury has rejected his assertion that his killing of his wife was unpremeditated.

How might the narrator be viewed as a cold-blooded killer tell-ing a false story to deny his true guilt?

This approach to the tale was discussed in the "Reading to Write" section. If you view the narrator as lying to conceal his crime, then much of what he says appears in a whole new light. His professed terror, bewilderment, and remorse are all calculated poses. What picture do you now form of this man? On the other hand, his narrative contains clues that expose his guilt. Does this suggest that some force like a conscience is working in him after all? And what of his introductory remarks, challenging readers to find a logical explanation for his tale: Are they the product of cool bravado or an uncon-scious wish to be found out?

Form and Genre

As a magazine editor as well as a writer, Poe was deeply immersed in the literature of his day, and he adopted many popular forms in his own stories. What is often problematic for readers is to decide whether he was presenting these forms in earnest, parodying them, or doing something in between. "The Black Cat" resembles a traditional ghost story and in some respects a temperance tale designed to expose the evils of alcohol-ism. Yet the tale somehow feels different from either of these. How is it different, and why?

Sample Topics:

1. **"The Black Cat" as ghost story:** One very common type of ghost story involves the return from death of a murder victim to avenge his or her own killing. Does Poe's story fit this genre? Would it be more accurate to describe the tale as appropriating the conventions of the ghost story to create a different effect?

An essay on this topic might begin by pointing out the simi-larities, not only in plot but in the focus placed on the terror experienced by the ghost's victim. You should go on, however, to consider the ways in which Poe's tale either expands or sub-verts the genre. On the one hand, the psychological dimension invites readers to think of the cat as embodying the narrator's own conscience. The parapraxis reinforces the interpretation that it is less a ghost than the conscience of the murderer that brings his undoing. On the other hand, the narrator might be playing up the supernatural to disguise the plain facts surrounding his wife's murder.

2. **"The Black Cat" as temperance literature:** Periodicals in Poe's time were filled with cautionary tales in which alcohol abuse led to destruction. In what way is "The Black Cat" related to this literature?

An essay on this topic, based on research into this body of literature, could describe the features of such stories and discuss their appearance in "The Black Cat." Consider how these features are used in Poe's tale. Is the tale an earnest demonstration of the evil effects of alcohol? Is the temperance message a cynical sop to attract readers? Is it an attempt by the narrator to win either the approval or the sympathy of the reader by casting himself as either a crusader against the evils of alcohol or one of its unfortunate victims? From a slightly different perspective, could the tale be an ironic jab at temperance literature itself—a way of suggesting that writing that trades on this emotionally laden topic diverts attention from deeper truths?

3. **The mystery as game:** In his first paragraph, the narrator pointedly suggests that there is a logical explanation for the events he relates. How might the tale be read as a contest in which the narrator challenges the reader to guess his secret?

There is considerable evidence that the narrator may have killed his wife deliberately at the time he claims to have killed his cat. If the story is read in this way, then the narrator's remarks seem to challenge the reader to find him out. In so doing, he treats us as he does the policemen, consciously trying to convince us of his (relative) innocence while another part of him acts to reveal his true crime. An essay could examine passages in which the narrator's writing helps arouse your suspicions. Examples include his excessive emotion in describing the killing of his cat, his preposterous explanation for the appearance of the figure of the cat in the bedroom wall, and his seemingly awkward use of the impersonal passive voice in describing the event on the cellar stairs.

From a literary standpoint, the tale enacts the kind of contest between writer and reader that lies at the heart of the mystery genre. The writer's job, as the detective novelist S. S. Van Dine has described it, is to present readers with a puzzle that they are unable to solve, despite being given all the clues necessary for solution. An essay could describe how such a contest emerges in "The Black Cat" and the thought process of the reader in trying to solve it.

Compare and Contrast Essays

Writers frequently return in their work to particular ideas or images. Examining such recurring motifs can be fascinating. Two examples are suggested below. In considering them, look closely not only at the specific motif but at the context in which it is used. Whether it is the image of an eye or the idea of a perverse impulse in man, what is interesting is not the thing in itself but what the author does with it, how the story treats it.

Sample Topics:

1. **Comparing "The Black Cat" to "The Imp of the Perverse":** Both tales refer explicitly to "perverseness," and both involve men who commit murders and are subsequently instrumental in exposing their own crimes. Discuss how the concept of perversity is treated in these tales.

An essay on this topic would go beyond merely discussing how each narrator describes "perverseness." The narrators in both tales have similar experiences, and both see themselves as victims of the same force. They tell their stories, however, in quite different ways. One goes into vivid, even gruesome detail, while the other recounts his tale in the sketchiest terms and almost as a mere addendum to a philosophical essay. One seems dispassionate and claims to understand exactly what has befallen him, while the other expresses terrified bewilderment. How do such differences in structure and tone affect the reader, particularly in terms of the concept of perverseness? How does your reading of one story affect your reading of the other?

2. **Comparing "eyes":** In carving out his cat's eye, the narrator resembles the man in "The Tell-Tale Heart," who fixates on his employer's eye. Discuss the image of the eye in these two works.

This topic is discussed in the chapter on "The Tell-Tale Heart."

Bibliography and Online Resources for "The Black Cat"

Amper, Susan. "Untold Story: The Lying Narrator in 'The Black Cat.'" *Studies in Short Fiction* 29 (1992): 475–85.

Bonaparte, Marie. "The Black Cat." *Partisan Review* 17 (1950): 834–60.

Crisman, William. "'Mere Household Events' in Poe's 'The Black Cat.'" *Studies in American Fiction* 12 (1984): 87–90.

Gargano, James. "'The Black Cat': Perverseness Reconsidered." *Texas Studies in Language and Literature* 2 (1960): 172–78.

Halliburton, David. *Edgar Allan Poe: A Phenomenological View.* Princeton, NJ: Princeton UP, 1973.

Hoffman, Daniel. "A Series of Mere Household Events." *Poe, Poe, Poe, Poe, Poe, Poe, Poe.* Garden City, NY: Doubleday, 1972. 233–42.

Lender, Mark Edward, and James Kirby Martin. *Drinking in America: A History.* New York: Free Press, 1987.

Matheson, T. J. "Poe's 'The Black Cat' as Critique of Temperance Literature." *Mosaic* 19 (1986): 69–81.

Reynolds, David S. "Black Cats and Delirium Tremens." *The Serpent in the Cup: Temperance in American Literature.* Ed. David S. Reynolds and Debra J. Rosenthal. Amherst: U of Massachusetts P, 1997. 22–59.

Van Dine, S. S. "Twenty Rules for Writing Detective Stories." 1928. Retrieved May 23, 2007. <http://gaslight.mtroyal.ab.ca/vandine.htm>.

"THE TELL-TALE HEART"

READING TO WRITE

"THE TELL-TALE Heart" begins with a question: "Why *will* you say that I am mad?" The narrator's ensuing monologue seems like an account of his insane murder of an old man. He speaks excitedly, describes behavior that seems purposeless, and claims to hear things. In addition, the reason he gives for the murder seems insane. These factors lead most readers unhesitatingly to believe the narrator mad.

Yet the story is by no means simple. For while there is much that suggests madness in the narrator's behavior—talking about the evil eye, shining the lantern, hearing the deathwatches, digging up the old man's body—it is unclear how the pieces fit together. Is the narrator insanely fearful of the old man's eye? Yet he connects his deepest terrors with the sound of the deathwatches in the wall. Are these two fears connected? He says that he is hypersensitive to sound, but hearing the beating of a dead man's heart is not hypersensitive but delusional. Has his guilty conscience driven him to uncover the man's body? But this is a response to what he has done: How is it related to the madness that brought about the crime in the first place? The reader seeks a unified theory that will bring these diverse elements together—unified, that is, in terms of either logic or psychology or even literary meaning.

One strategy is to start by considering the evil eye. This is the motive the narrator gives for the murder. What can it mean, or what might it represent on a metaphorical level? Whatever you believe the eye represents could be the source of the young man's fear. In this way, you can discuss the nature of his madness. To take one example, if the eye represents something always looking at him—conscience—then the young man's madness might be viewed in terms of an overactive, punishing conscience and his murder of the old man as an attempt to escape from that conscience.

Another approach is to view the old man and the narrator as psychological doubles representing two parts of the human self or mind. This viewpoint is suggested by comments the narrator makes that explicitly link him and the old man. The narrator sees the old man's fears on the night of the murder as identical to his own. Might he be driven to murder by the irrational belief that by killing the old man he can destroy his own debilitating fears?

Alternatively, the age difference and the fact that the two men live together suggest an interpretation of them as father and son. Considering the murder as a patricide introduces a new set of psychological and psychosexual interpretations. Ponder, too, what is suggested by the unique manner in which the murder is committed: a murder by mattress.

One way to account for the apparent inconsistencies in the tale is to conclude that the narrator is lying. His story is, after all, the account of a man who has just been caught in a murder. He cannot deny that he committed the crime, so what defense can he offer? He can pretend to be insane. In this case, it should not be surprising if the parts of his story do not quite mesh into a convincing whole. The historical context of Poe's tale supports such a reading, for at the time the story appeared, the use—and abuse—of the insanity defense was a prominent public issue.

To see how some of the themes emerge in the story, consider this passage, in which the narrator discusses his motive for the murder:

> It is impossible to say how first the idea entered my brain; but once conceived, it haunted me day and night. Object there was none. Passion there was none. I loved the old man. He had never wronged me. He had never given me insult. For his gold I had no desire. I think it was his eye! yes, it was this! One of his eyes resembled that of a vulture—a pale blue eye, with a film over it. Whenever it fell upon me, my blood ran cold; and so by degrees—very gradually—I made up my mind to take the life of the old man, and thus rid myself of the eye forever!

Placed near the start, this passage points the way to what the tale will be about. Yet in a few sentences the passage manages to point in several directions. As the speaker explains his motive, look for clues about what is driving this man. When he seems to settle on the matter of the old man's eye, scrutinize his description of it in an attempt to tease out its significance. Does it represent parental authority, mortality, the eye of God, or the evil eye that can inflict harm on others? Scholars have put forward all of these interpretations.

Some readers find such interpretations unsatisfying, because they feel either that the story provides too little substance to support these theories or that too much of the focus of the tale lies elsewhere. Returning to the passage, search for other possible starting points. One is the statement, "I loved the old man." Following this thread, consider the narrator's comments about sharing the old man's terror, the manner in which the murder is accomplished, and the young man's passionate exposure of his own crime. Does a focus on the young man's feelings for his victim provide an effective way to organize the tale?

Careful readers will notice, too, that the man's comments in the passage are self-contradictory. At first he claims that he had no motive at all, and a moment later he states emphatically that his motive was to destroy the man's eye. Adding to the peculiarity, he says that he "think[s]" it was his eye and then says, "[Y]es, it was this!" as if the idea has just come to him. How can that be, when he says that the eye had bothered him for so long? Finally, his first sentence says that the idea of killing the man haunted him day and night once it was conceived; the last sentence says the opposite, that the decision came to him "very gradually."

As a reader, try to make sense of these contradictions. Are they evidence of his mental confusion or of his duplicity? People in real life often seek to conceal their motives. Perhaps the doubtful way the narrator introduces the idea of the old man's eye should be a signal that this is not his real reason at all. In that case, what is the reason? Is it one of the motives he has just denied? Here, too, search for clues in what follows. Doing so will reveal two subsequent references to the man's money.

Finally, if he is trying to deceive, perhaps he is not mad after all. The way he dismembers the body is quite sensible. The policemen do not treat him as mad; on the contrary, they mock his seemingly insane behavior. Here, as before, examine the rest of the tale to see how well the theory fits.

In one brief introductory paragraph Poe sets many trails for you to follow as you read.

TOPICS AND STRATEGIES
Themes

Following the path that you began in the preceding section, search through the story to trace how a theme develops as the tale progresses. One strategy involves focusing on the sources of the young man's apparent madness, such as the old man's eye. An equally valid approach is to consider the nature of the narrator's behavior and what this may be saying about his mental state.

Sample Topics:

1. **Guilt:** The narrator commits a murder. What ideas does the story raise about his guilt, and what attitudes toward his guilt does the story engender in the reader?

   Many readers see the narrator as driven to commit murder by feelings of guilt; this idea is discussed in the section on character. A related approach is to consider what ideas the story raises about the nature of guilt and people's attitude toward it. What feelings does the story elicit toward the narrator's madness and his crime? Are you fascinated, repulsed, sympathetic? What in the narrator's situation or behavior gives rise to these feelings? Might the narrator be knowingly manipulating the reader in this respect? An essay on this topic could consider, in addition to the preceding, the question of how people weigh a person's guilt. If the narrator is mad—or a victim, as he suggests, of uncontrollable fears—is he less blameworthy? If his conscience drives him to reveal his crime, should that mitigate his punishment? What if the revelation is driven instead by delusion? What if it is driven by the hope of escaping punishment—by the belief that the police will soon discover the crime anyway? The man's situation raises such questions: Does the tale seem to offer any answers?

2. **Mental illness:** If the narrator is mad, what are the nature and causes of his madness? How does the tale treat the idea of madness?

This topic invites several approaches. One is to attempt to identify the nature of the man's madness. Does his behavior fit the symptoms of any recognized form of mental illness, such as paranoia or obsessive-compulsive disorder? After showing such connections, an essay could draw connections between what is generally thought to cause such illness and the situation of the narrator.

Readers who decide that the narrator's behavior does not fit any known illness are left with a set of behaviors to try to make sense of. The man's obsession with the evil eye, his hypersensitivity to sound, his fevered imagining that he hears the beating of the dead man's heart—what do they all amount to? Is the tale presenting a grab bag of extreme mental states, and if so, to what effect? Is it merely playing on our emotions? Is it slyly commenting on the gullibility of the public or its taste for sensationalism?

Still another approach would be to explore the tale's apparent attitude toward the man's mental state. To what extent do you identify with his comments about the terrors he has felt in the night? To what extent do you take enjoyment in observing his madness? At one point he says, "I knew what the old man felt, and pitied him, although I chuckled at heart." How well does this statement describe the experience of the reader? What does this suggest about our attitudes toward mental illness?

Finally, what ideas does the story suggest about madness and rationality? The narrator insists that his extreme nervousness is not proof of madness—that, on the contrary, his methodical behavior proves his sanity. An essay on this topic would analyze specifically the grounds on which readers judge the man mad. Are the shining of the lantern, the dismemberment of the body, and the subsequent revealing of the body equally mad? They do not appear to be equally irrational. Such analysis can form the basis for a discussion of what constitutes sanity and insanity, and how we make judgments on the question.

3. **Time:** How does the tale activate the themes of time and mortality, and what ideas does it suggest about these themes?

References to time and clocks abound in the story and are frequently linked with references to death. An essay could collect and discuss these numerous references. Is the narrator himself obsessed with time? He says that he has lain awake, night after night, listening to the "death-watches," a kind of beetle, in the wall. Is he abnormally fearful of death or the passage of time? He suggests that he sees his victim as an older version of himself. Is the murder intended to erase a constant reminder of his own mortality?

Character

The principal character in the tale commits a grisly murder. The first focus is likely to be what has driven him to this crime. If you accept his word that he did not act from such ordinary motives as money or revenge, you will seek to understand him in terms of abnormal psychological forces.

The principle that characters are revealed by their actions and words applies in a special way to a first-person narrator, since the story itself is the product of his character. In "The Tell-Tale Heart" the narrator's emotional style of writing might be considered evidence of his mental state. You should also weigh the circumstances under which he is writing. He is presumably under arrest for his crime. Do not assume that he will tell us the truth.

Sample Topics:

1. **Guilt and fear:** The narrator's chief attribute, or what motivates him, seems to be guilt or fear. Discuss one or both of these emotions in terms of the narrator's mental state and behavior.

The narrator acknowledges experiencing extreme terror. Feelings of guilt may be inferred from his abhorrence of the old man's eye. A good essay can be written identifying either of these qualities, discussing how it is revealed in the character, explaining how it affects his behavior, and perhaps speculating on the possible sources of the emotion in the man's personal history.

2. **The narrator as sane:** Is it possible that the narrator is only feigning madness? How might the story support such a reading?

Modern readers readily conclude, based on the narrator's words and actions, that he is mad. If you consider the context of the man's story, however, you might adopt a more skeptical viewpoint. He has committed murder and has been caught red-handed. What other defense can he offer but insanity? It is true that he claims to be sane, yet everything in his tale makes him appear mad. Has he expressly designed it to have that effect? The only third-person evidence in the story is the reaction of the policemen to his raving and foaming. What is suggested by their calm and "mocking" response?

3. **The doppelganger:** A doppelganger is a person's double, who is seen as shadowing or haunting the character in some way. How might the old man be viewed as the narrator's doppelganger?

An essay on this topic would first establish a correlation between the two characters. The narrator closely identifies with the old man, observing that they have both experienced the same sensations. It is also possible in the second paragraph of the tale to infer a link from the close conjunction of the old man's "eye" with the pronoun "I," referring to the narrator. Once a connection between the two men is made, it would be interesting to explore the nature of the fear or loathing that the old man inspires in the narrator. Viewed from a psychological perspective, is there something in himself that the young man wishes to extinguish?

History and Context

Placing a tale in its context requires dexterity on the part of the essayist. Readers demand that literature speak to all ages, yet writers inescapably are the products of their culture and times. The resulting tension is particularly prominent in the work of Poe, who on the one hand seems focused on essential struggles of the human soul but on the other hand, as a magazine editor and writer, immersed himself in contemporary culture. "The Tell-Tale Heart," in many ways timeless, is very much a story of its day. At the time it was written, the situation of a murderer whose sanity is open to question played directly to one of the decade's hottest controversies. The tale may draw, too, on popular superstition regarding the supposed powers of the evil eye. Essays are most successful when they provide sufficient research and insight into the relevant context, while leaving room for more universal interpretation.

1. **The insanity defense:** Around the time the tale was published, magazines and newspapers were filled with writings about the controversial new use of the insanity defense. How does this context affect your reading of the tale?

   By 1840 trials featuring insanity defenses were major media events. To write on this topic, you would first research the controversy and the legal, moral, and philosophical issues that it raised. One approach would be to select one or more specific issues in the debate and draw connections between these issues and elements in Poe's tale.

   The context is also relevant to the view of the narrator as feigning insanity (see the "Character" section), for much of the controversy centered on the abuse of the insanity defense, which had led to acquittals in several notorious cases in which the defendants appeared to be perfectly sane. An essay could explain how in this context, readers would have approached the tale and its narrator more skeptically in Poe's time than they do today.

2. **The evil eye:** Superstition regarding the evil eye was widespread in Poe's time. How are popular ideas on the subject reflected in the tale?

   Much research is available on the topic of the evil eye. (See, for example, Frederick Elworthy, *The Evil Eye: The Classic Account of an Evil Superstition*.) One popular superstition was that an individual possessing an evil eye was capable of inflicting injury on those at whom he directed it. How does the story adopt and use such ideas, and what part does this treatment play in the story as a whole?

Another approach is to trace the appearance of the evil eye in literature, particularly in gothic novels such as Ann Radcliffe's *The Italian* (1797) and Charles Maturin's *Melmoth the Wanderer* (1820). Secondary sources, such as Alan Dundes's *The Evil Eye: A Casebook,* might help you identify relevant works. To what extent does Poe follow in the footsteps of earlier works, and in what ways does he turn the traditional image to his own purposes?

3. **Poe and money:** What connections might be made between Poe's tale and his personal financial concerns?

Though the narrator discounts money as a motive in the murder, his phrasing at this point is peculiar. In addition, the old man's money is mentioned at least twice again in the tale. Could money be more important to the narrator and to the tale than the young man admits? Money appears as a seemingly subordinate element in a great many of Poe's other tales and was an overriding concern in his life. An essay on this topic might explore the concealed importance of money in the tale and connect this with biographical information regarding Poe's crushing financial woes.

Compare and Contrast Essays

"The Tell-Tale Heart" is almost a prototype of the psychological tale of terror. As such, it invites comparison not only with other Poe tales but with a body of fiction stretching all the way to today's latest thriller about a serial killer. Comparisons can be made at any point along this trail of literary evolution. In most cases, the interesting questions concern what has remained the same and what has changed, in either content or form.

Sample Topics:

1. **Comparing "The Tell-Tale Heart" to a modern horror story:** Compare the themes, imagery, or style of Poe's tale to those in a modern short story, film, or graphic novel.

You can compare the elements of the two works, the effects the works create, and the relationship between elements and effects. Do the two works use similar methods, or do they create feelings of terror in different ways? Does the modern work raise psychological issues similar to those in "The Tell-Tale Heart"? Are there counterparts to Poe's provocative imagery, such as the old man's evil eye, the watch enveloped in cotton, and the peculiar murder by bed?

2. **Comparing narrators:** Poe's stories are often told in the first person. Compare one or more other first-person Poe narrators to the narrator of "The Tell-Tale Heart."

The narrator of "Ligeia" appears awestruck. That of "The Black Cat" professes to be bewildered. Montresor in "The Cask of Amontillado" appears cool and amused. An essay might explore their respective attitudes. How sincere is the emotion each displays? Are they all posing? To what extent and for what purpose? In what ways do the narrators attempt to elicit the sympathy or otherwise manipulate the emotions of their readers? An essay might also examine how the tale raises these issues. How does it manage to reveal aspects of the narrators' characters that the narrators—the storytellers themselves—try to hide?

3. **Comparing eyes:** The young man's fixation on his victim's eye finds a striking parallel in the "The Black Cat." Discuss the image of the eye in these two works.

To write on this topic, first reflect on what the eye might represent. This involves thinking about the image of an eye and also examining how the eye is referred to in each work. How do the old man's eye and the cat's activate either fear or hatred in their respective assassins? This question might lead you to consider more broadly the relationship between each narrator and his victim as well as each narrator's psychological state.

4. **Comparing the murder and the cleanup.** The narrator boasts about how cleverly he accomplishes both of these actions. Discuss the similarities and differences and what they imply about the narrator.

The narrator speaks of the two actions in similar ways, and readers tend to see both actions as obsessive. On reflection, however, the concealment of the body, unlike the seemingly pointless shining of the lantern, appears quite purposeful and effective. Does it seem mad because a man in this state ought not be so calm and collected? Or is the narrator leading his readers into thinking him mad when he is not? It is possible to take this line of thought a step further. If the two actions really are comparable, and if the concealment is logical, might there likewise be a logical explanation for the lantern shining? What might the narrator really have been doing for the eight nights leading up to the murder?

Bibliography for "The Tell-Tale Heart"

Bynum, Paige-Matthey. "'Observe How Healthily—How Calmly I Tell You the Whole Story': Moral Insanity and Edgar Allan Poe's 'The Tell-Tale Heart.'" *Literature and Science as Modes of Expression*. Ed. Frederick Amrine. Boston: Kluwer Academic Publishers, 1989. 141–52.

Canario, John W. "The Dream in 'The Tell-Tale Heart.'" *English Language Notes* 7 (1970): 194–97.

Cleman, John. "Irresistible Impulses: Edgar Allan Poe and the Insanity Defense." *American Literature* 63 (1991): 623–40.

Dundes, Alan. *The Evil Eye: A Casebook*. Madison: U of Wisconsin P, 1992.

Elworthy, Frederick Thomas. *The Evil Eye: The Classic Account of an Evil Superstition*. New York: Dover Publications, 2004.

Frank, F. S. "Neighborhood Gothic: Poe's 'The Tell-Tale Heart.'" *The Sphinx: A Magazine of Literature and Society* 3 (1981): 53–60.

Gargano, James W. "The Theme of Time in 'The Tell-Tale Heart.'" *Studies in Short Fiction* 5 (1968): 378–82.

Geary, Rick. "The Tell-Tale Heart." *Graphic Classics Volume I: Edgar Allan Poe*. Mount Horeb, WI: Eureka Productions, 2006. 4–22.

Hoffman, Daniel. *Poe Poe Poe Poe Poe Poe Poe.* Garden City, NY: Doubleday, 1972.

Ketterer, David. *The Rationale of Deception in Poe.* Baton Rouge: Louisiana State UP, 1979.

Kirkland, James. "'The Tell-Tale Heart' as Evil Eye Event." *Southern Folklore* 56 (1999): 135–47.

Phillips, Elizabeth. "Mere Household Events: The Metaphysics of Mania." *Edgar Allan Poe: An American Imagination.* New York: Kennikat, 1979. 97–137.

Poe, Edgar Allan. "Edgar Allan Poe's Contributions to *Alexander's Weekly Messenger.*" *Proceedings of the American Antiquarian Society.* Ed. Clarence S. Brigham. Worcester, MA: American Antiquarian Society, 1943. 105–06.

Reilly, J. "The Lesser Death-Watch and 'The Tell-Tale Heart.'" *ATQ* 2 (1969): 3–9.

Robinson, E. Arthur. "Poe's 'The Tell-Tale Heart.'" *Nineteenth Century Fiction* 19 (1965): 369–78.

Silverman, Kenneth. *Edgar A. Poe: Mournful and Never-Ending Remembrance.* New York: Harper Collins, 1991.

Tucker, B. D. "'The Tell-Tale Heart' and the 'Evil Eye.'" *Southern Literary Journal* 13, no. 2 (1981): 92–98.

Zimmerman, Brett. "'Moral Insanity' or Paranoid Schizophrenia: Poe's 'The Tell-Tale Heart.'" *Mosaic* 25 (1992): 39–48.

"THE PURLOINED
LETTER"

READING TO WRITE

"The Purloined Letter" is the third of Poe's stories featuring the detective C. Auguste Dupin. In having created these tales, Poe is credited with inventing the genre of detective fiction. "The Purloined Letter" includes a number of features that characterize this genre, such as the characters of detective, sidekick, policeman, and archvillain, as well as the use of first-person narration. Detective fiction is an enduring genre that has evolved into a web of related subgenres, and to this day it seems only to grow in popularity. "The Purloined Letter" offers you an almost limitless range of possibilities for connecting to this body of literature.

In one respect, however, Poe's tale differs markedly from most later detective stories: It does not allow the reader to participate in guessing the perpetrator or how the crime was committed. The tale does present a puzzle in the matter of where the minister has hidden the queen's letter, but it does not provide a trail of clues for readers to follow along with the detective. The tale centers instead on the detective's lengthy commentary regarding the nature of analytical thinking. This intellectual discourse, consuming about half of the story, raises questions for readers. Does the tale mean to be more a philosophical tract than a work of fiction? Does it mean to be profound, and if so, does it succeed? What is the relationship between the fictional story and the ideas in the tale? Does the story illustrate the ideas? Do Dupin's explanations reveal his character? If readers respond by being confused about the aims or design of the tale, in what way could that confusion be part of the tale's design?

Consider two excerpts from this tale. The first appears near the beginning, with the arrival of the prefect of police. The narrator, the nameless friend of Dupin, writes:

> We gave him a hearty welcome; for there was nearly half as much of the entertaining as of the contemptible about the man, and we had not seen him for several years. We had been sitting in the dark, and Dupin now arose for the purpose of lighting a lamp, but sat down again, without doing so, upon G.'s saying that he had called to consult us, or rather to ask the opinion of my friend, about some official business which had occasioned a great deal of trouble.
>
> "If it is any point requiring reflection," observed Dupin, as he forebore to enkindle the wick, "we shall examine it to better purpose in the dark."
>
> "That is another of your odd notions," said the Prefect, who had a fashion of calling every thing "odd" that was beyond his comprehension, and thus lived amid an absolute legion of "oddities."
>
> "Very true," said Dupin, as he supplied his visiter with a pipe, and rolled towards him a comfortable chair.
>
> "And what is the difficulty now?" I asked. "Nothing more in the assassination way, I hope?"
>
> "Oh no; nothing of that nature. The fact is, the business is very simple indeed, and I make no doubt that we can manage it sufficiently well ourselves; but then I thought Dupin would like to hear the details of it, because it is so excessively *odd*."
>
> "Simple and odd," said Dupin.
>
> "Why, yes; and not exactly that, either. The fact is, we have all been a good deal puzzled because the affair *is* so simple, and yet baffles us altogether."
>
> "Perhaps it is the very simplicity of the thing which puts you at fault," said my friend.
>
> "What nonsense you *do* talk!" replied the Prefect, laughing heartily.

This passage is most noteworthy in terms of the way that it establishes the characters in the tale and their interrelationship. Although the overall tone is pleasant, a careful reading reveals rivalry and tension among the three men. The narrator introduces the prefect as "entertaining" and "despicable," words that suggest considerable condescension on the narrator's part. The conversation about thinking in the dark suggests in just a few sentences the attitudes of all three men toward one another. The prefect dismisses Dupin's idea as an "odd notion" without seriously considering it. The narrator in turn gibes that the prefect calls everything odd that he does not understand—which amounts to a great many things. On the one hand, you might agree with the narrator's assessment of the prefect's intelligence, or at least his intellectual curiosity. On the other hand, you might note that the narrator's remark is the second insult he has directed at the prefect in some four sentences. What, you might ask, is his problem with the prefect?

While the narrator bristles at the prefect's remark, Dupin ignores it completely. Offering no explanation or rationale for his idea, he simply agrees with the prefect and offers him a pipe and a chair. This might be a sign that Dupin likes the prefect and wishes to be polite and pleasant. Alternatively, Dupin might consider himself too far above the prefect to bother responding to him or trying to enlighten him.

Examine along similar lines the subsequent exchange regarding Dupin's idea that the simplicity of the case is what makes it difficult. The entire tale may be mined for further clues, because the personalities of these characters (along with the minister) and especially the interrelations among them are major elements in the tale. Indeed, these characters are prototypes for similar characters who can be found throughout the huge body of detective fiction that Poe's work has spawned.

It is useful to consider your own reaction to the men's exchanges. Do you find yourself sharing the narrator's judgment of the prefect? Or do you distance yourself from both the prefect and the narrator? What is your attitude toward Dupin's idea about thinking in the dark? Is it an "odd notion"? Or rather a concept too deep for dull minds like the prefect's? Such questions come back in force in the second half of the tale, when Dupin begins to explain his methods and ideas. The following example presents his comments about the limitations of mathematical reasoning.

"In short, I never yet encountered the mere mathematician who could be trusted out of equal roots, or one who did not clandestinely hold it as a point of his faith that $x^2 + px$ was absolutely and unconditionally equal to q.

Say to one of these gentlemen, by way of experiment, if you please, that you believe occasions may occur where $x^2 + px$ is *not* altogether equal to q, and, having made him understand what you mean, get out of his reach as speedily as convenient, for, beyond doubt, he will endeavor to knock you down.

"I mean to say," continued Dupin, while I merely laughed at his last observations, "that if the Minister had been no more than a mathematician, the Prefect would have been under no necessity of giving me this check. I knew him, however, as both mathematician and poet, and my measures were adapted to his capacity, with reference to the circumstances by which he was surrounded. I knew him as a courtier, too, and a bold *intriguant.* Such a man, I considered, could not fail to be aware of the ordinary policial modes of action. He could not have failed to anticipate—and events have proved that he did not fail to anticipate—the waylayings to which he was subjected. He must have foreseen, I reflected, the secret investigations of his premises."

How do you react to Dupin's discussion? Some of it is very esoteric, while the basic idea seems quite simple. Obviously, the police were going to search the minister's premises thoroughly. Obviously, the minister had to think of a hiding place they would not think of. Has Dupin, then, really done anything brilliant? In fairness, he does not expressly claim to be brilliant, although he implies that he is smarter than either the prefect or the minister. Does his lengthy explanation make him seem smart or pompous or both? It is curious that the narrator admits that he laugh at some of what Dupin says. Is he laughing only at the amusing way Dupin expresses himself at that moment? Or does his laugh connect him with the dimwitted prefect, who laughs at Dupin in the passage at the start of the story? In short, do not assume that the story is presenting Dupin and his ideas entirely in earnest. Instead, the tale seems at every turn to challenge you to decide for yourself how brilliant he is, how profound, and even how sincere.

TOPICS AND STRATEGIES
Character
Dupin discusses the prefect and the minister, as well as himself, mostly in terms of how they think. This is one important part of their makeup, but readers should also consider other clues.

Each of these characters, to an extent Poe could not have imagined, has become iconic. They represent models, almost amounting to stock characters, in succeeding generations of detective stories: the sidekick, who is often the narrator; the policeman, who ranges from decent fellow of limited ability to overbearing bumbler; the archenemy, as brilliant—or almost—as the detective; and of course the detective himself, brilliant but eccentric. It is worthwhile to consider what makes these characters so enduring.

About Dupin there is more to be said. As we have just discussed, there are grounds for questioning his absolute brilliance. Even more question-able are his motivations. Readers will benefit from a close and hard look at Dupin, for flawed and ambiguous characters tend to be both more true to life and more interesting.

Sample Topics:

1. **Dupin as detective:** Poe's leading character in this tale is the model of the master detective. How would you describe his persona?

   An essay on this topic would consider Dupin's analytical meth-ods and manner. His words and actions in particular might be examined for what they indicate about his self-image and his relationships with other people.

   Dupin's immediate successor, Sherlock Holmes, resembles him almost embarrassingly closely. In other classic detectives, including Agatha Christie's Hercule Poirot, Rex Stout's Nero Wolfe, and many others, Dupin's features are changed, but much of his essence remains. To what extent is such resemblance nat-ural or even inevitable? After all, these detectives must share special mental faculties if they are to solve crimes that others cannot. Consider which aspects of Dupin's character would be difficult for other mystery writers to change and which would be easy. This topic also lends itself to a compare and contrast approach.

2. **Dupin as humbug:** Most readers share Dupin's own opin-ion that he is a genius. Is it possible to sketch an alternative interpretation?

First you might ask how brilliant Dupin has really been in concluding that the letter must be in plain sight. As he himself points out, any attempt at concealment would have been futile, so what choice did the minister have? And who has not at one time or other thought of a similar strategy? In fact, Dupin himself points to the idea that his genius may be less than it appears. Describing the schoolboy's trick of adopting the expression of his opponent as a way of guessing the opponent's thoughts, Dupin says that this method lies at the bottom of the "spurious profundity" of leading intellectuals. In so doing, does he not invite his hearers to regard his own profundity as spurious?

An analysis of this topic should also weigh Dupin's very lengthy explanations themselves. Perhaps the man is brilliant, perhaps only clever, but he is definitely long-winded. Are his prolonged explanations merely the product of his fascination with the workings of the mind, or do they also suggest a certain degree of pomposity and self-satisfaction?

3. **Dupin's moral character:** Fictional detectives are often regarded as crime fighters devoted to finding the truth and seeing that justice is done. How well does this image fit Auguste Dupin?

   An essay on this topic would examine Dupin's motivations. What role do his political allegiances and the offer of a reward play? What may be inferred from the fact that he keeps the letter for perhaps as long as a month before giving it to the police? To what extent does the note he leaves for the minister show him to be vengeful or vindictive?

4. **The prefect:** This character is an essential foil for Dupin. What does the prefect's behavior reveal about his mental abilities and limitations? In what ways does he emerge as more than just Dupin's inferior intellectual counterpart?

   Dupin describes the prefect as limited not in intelligence but in his intellectual viewpoint. Is that an accurate description?

Aside from his mental ability, what kind of person is he? At times he appears to condescend to Dupin. Does such behavior reflect fatuous self-satisfaction, hardheaded commonsense, or both?

5. **The minister:** Describe the character of the minister as revealed by his actions and as described by other characters.

Much of the focus on the minister's character, especially for Dupin, concerns his intelligence. Where does he fit in the hierarchy of intelligence established by Dupin, and what behavior reveals this? Aside from his intellect, what sort of person is he?

You might also discuss the minister, who is usually referred to as "D—," as a double or mirror image of Dupin. In what ways are they similar? In particular, Dupin describes the minister as "an unprincipled man of genius." How well does this description fit the minister? How well does it fit Dupin?

6. **The narrator:** What ideas can you form about the character of the narrator?

Unlike the other characters, the narrator is not described. Instead, you must use his own account to make inferences about him. When does he offer his opinions, and when does he refrain? How do others speak to him, and how does he respond? What do his descriptions of other characters reveal about him? From such bits of evidence, the narrator emerges as more than just an insignificant, colorless recorder of events.

It is useful, too, to consider the narrator in relation to the detective. To what extent do they counterpoint each other? Is it possible to read them as two halves of the human character?

Philosophy and Ideas

In writing about the ideas in a story, bear in mind that the stated ideas provide only a starting point for an essay. It is not enough to reiterate or paraphrase Dupin's ideas or to argue against them. Indeed, do not assume that Dupin's ideas are the same as Poe's or that Poe wrote the story to advance these ideas. The ideas, in short, are best read, like character or setting, as elements in a work of fiction.

A good essay will develop a point that the story itself does not state. Such a point might be that Dupin's ideas about mathematics and poetry reflect an attempt to bridge the divide between human intellect and emotion. Or you might argue that the story presents a conflict between Dupin's intellectual ideas and his much more emotional behavior.

Sample Topics:

1. **Ratiocination:** A large part of the tale is devoted to a discussion of reason. What ideas does the story offer regarding the nature and limits of human reason?

   To write an essay on this topic, begin by considering the ideas Dupin raises regarding the limited analysis of the prefect and the police, the limited applicability of mathematical reasoning, and so forth. It is important, however, to move beyond what Dupin himself says and consider his ideas in the context of the tale.

   Dupin's ideas can obviously be read in relation to his solution of the problem. But you might also view them in regard to other aspects of the tale. How are Dupin's mental process and his discussion of it related to his personality, motivations, and relationships with other characters?

   A number of questions might be asked. Is Dupin's behavior the product of pure intellectual analysis? Why does Dupin spend so much time explaining his ideas to the narrator, and why does the narrator spend so much time passing them on to the reader? Evidently, these men consider these ideas profoundly important. Does that reveal more about the ideas or more about the men?

2. **Power:** Both political and personal power figure prominently in the tale. Discuss how power is represented.

   The chief importance of the purloined letter lies in the political power it gives to the minister. Yet the tale also focuses on interpersonal power. A focused reading would uncover many references to the power or powerlessness of various characters. Intellectual methods and ability are repeatedly described in terms of the power they confer. Dupin's favorite illustrations of his ideas involve success in competitive games. What ideas do these references give you about the nature of power, its sources, its uses, and its role in interpersonal relations?

Form and Genre

A genre study can take many forms. Typically, you would examine specific features that typify the genre. You may choose any feature and approach it from one of several viewpoints.

In a historical approach, you would examine how the feature has evolved through the years. How has the character of the detective changed, or the character of the policeman? Has the nature of the crimes being detected remained largely the same, or has it changed in some identifiable way?

In a formalist-structuralist approach, you would study how a feature operates within the story. If the detective usually seems eccentric, why is this so? In many works, much is made of characters' alibis. How do these function in the mystery? How is it that some mysteries hardly concern themselves with alibis at all?

Clearly, there is a wide range of topics on which to write. There is also a great deal already written and easily accessible. Doing some library or Internet research would be helpful both in finding topic ideas and in getting a sense of how to develop them.

Sample Topics:

1. **The detective story:** In his Auguste Dupin tales, Poe is credited with having invented the detective story. Using "The Purloined Letter," describe and discuss the characteristic features of this genre.

   As noted above, begin by narrowing the topic, perhaps by choosing a specific feature of the genre on which to focus. You might concentrate on some aspect of plot structure, character, setting, or theme. One interesting approach is to consider a characteristic historically, the variations on the theme throughout detective fiction. You might survey the policeman character, for example, in a variety of detective stories. Another approach is to explore why a genre characteristic is the way it is. What might be the reason—either practical or artistic—that this tale (along with so many detective stories) is told in the first person by the sidekick? Clearly, looking at genres invites any number of compare and contrast essays, as discussed below.

2. **Narrative form:** The tale is written in such a way that what might be the most exciting scenes—the two thefts of the letter—are subordinated to lengthy conversation. Discuss the nature of this narrative design and the way it affects your reading of the tale.

You might begin by considering the features of the text that subordinate the action. First is sheer quantity: The tale devotes more space to the conversation than to the action. Equally important, the action is discussed in summary fashion, not in specific, immediate detail, and it is recounted at second and third hand.

The obvious question that follows is, Why is the tale designed in this way? Is it meant to be primarily about the ideas it expresses? Are they, then, so significant and profound? Is the trickster tale meant merely to illustrate the ideas? Or might you think of the tale as a story about men who like to spend their time discussing such ideas? Asking such questions may help you formulate a thesis about how the tale has been designed and why.

Compare and Contrast Essays

Generally speaking, there are two types of compare and contrast essays. In one, you would compare two or more things within the work being studied. In this case, the comparison may be thought of as part of the design of the tale. How does the contrast between the prefect and Dupin help show Dupin's strengths—and weaknesses? How do the similarities between Dupin and the minister help reveal the detective's darker side?

The second type of essay connects features of one work with comparable features of another. As noted in the "Form and Genre" section, Poe's Dupin stories have strongly influenced later works, and numerous elements of "The Purloined Letter" can be seen in similar form in detective fiction ever since. In making comparisons of this kind, an essay should go beyond the mere fact of similarity or difference. You should also suggest a reason. In discussing similarities, you might suggest why the similar elements are so enduring or what common theme they support. Alternatively, you might discuss how the differences create different effects or how they reflect different cultural conditions when the respective works were written.

Sample Topics:

1. **Comparing the two thefts.** First the minister steals the letter from the queen. Subsequently, Dupin steals it from the minister. Discuss these two acts and their interconnection.

   An essay on this topic could discuss the methods of the minister and Dupin, along with the key ideas of concealment and exposure and of what the respective characters see and fail to see. You might also discuss the changing roles of the characters. It has been said that in the first scene the king does not see; the queen sees that the king does not see and therefore mistakenly believes she is safe; and the minister sees the true situation and is able to exploit it. Could it be said that in the second theft, the relationships among the prefect, the minister, and Dupin create a similar pattern?

2. **Comparing characters:** Dupin compares his own intellectual approach with that of other characters. What other comparisons can be made between and among the four men?

   An essay on this topic should go beyond what Dupin himself says about the prefect's understanding, the minister's, and his own. You could compare two characters or more, examining their personalities and moral character as well as their intellect. Examine the characters' statements and behavior as well as what is said about them. You might describe a continuum from the prefect to the narrator to the minister to Dupin; or you might pair the prefect with the narrator and the minister with Dupin, or the narrator with Dupin. Explaining such choices and the reasons on which they are based could make a thought-provoking essay.

3. **Comparing mystery tales:** Compare one or more aspects of "The Purloined Letter" with similar features in another detective story or novel.

The choice of possible approaches here is almost endless. You could compare Poe's tale to a close relative, such as a Sherlock Holmes story, or to a variation on the genre, such as the "hardboiled" detective stories of Raymond Chandler or Dashiell Hammett. You can compare characters, focusing on either the detectives or other characters. Or you might examine such structural matters as the order in which the mystery unfolds, the methods of detection, or how suspense is maintained. Narrative style and setting also make good topics.

Bibliography and Online Resources for "The Purloined Letter"

Asselineau, Roger. "Edgar Allan Poe." *American Writers*. Vol. 3. Ed. Jay Parini. New York: Charles Scribner's Sons, 1977. 409–32.

Babener, Lianha Klenman. "The Shadow's Shadow: The Motif of the Double in Edgar Allan Poe's 'The Purloined Letter.'" *The Purloined Poe*. Ed. John P. Muller and William J. Richardson. Baltimore: Johns Hopkins UP, 1988. 323–34.

Bonaparte, Marie. *The Life and Works of Edgar Allan Poe: A Psycho-analytic Interpretation*. Trans. John Rodker. 1949. Reprint, New York: Humanities Press, 1971.

Buranelli, Vincent. "Chapter 4: Fiction Themes." 1978. *Edgar Allan Poe: Twayne's United States Authors Series Online*. G. K. Hall, 1999.

Carlson, E. W., ed. *The Recognition of Edgar Allan Poe: Selected Criticism since 1829*. Ann Arbor: U of Michigan P, 1966.

Crisman, William. "Poe's Dupin as Professional, the Dupin Stories as Serial Text." *Studies in American Fiction* 23 (Autumn 1995): 215–29.

Holland, Norman N. "Re-covering 'The Purloined Letter': Reading as a Personal Transaction." *The Purloined Poe.* Ed. John P. Muller and William J. Richardson. Baltimore: Johns Hopkins UP, 1988. 285–306.

Irwin, John T. "Mysteries We Reread: Mysteries of Rereading." *MLN* 101, no. 5 (1986): 1,168–215.

Johnson, Barbara. "The Frame of Reference: Poe, Lacan, Derrida." *The Purloined Poe.* Ed. John P. Muller and William J. Richardson. Baltimore: Johns Hopkins UP, 1988. 213–51.

Peraldi, Francois. "A Note on Time in 'The Purloined Letter.'" *The Purloined Poe.* Ed. John P. Muller and William J. Richardson. Baltimore: Johns Hopkins UP, 1988. 335–42.

Van Dine, S. S. "Twenty Rules for Writing Detective Stories." Available online. URL: http://gaslight.mtroyal.ab.ca/vandine.htm. Updated on Jan. 11, 2000. Originally published in *American Magazine,* 1928.

"THE CASK OF AMONTILLADO"

READING TO WRITE

"THE CASK of Amontillado" is considered by many critics to be Poe's finest tale. A chilling plot weaves themes tied to character, setting, and a haunting narrative voice. The interplay of these elements provides a rich field for essay writing.

The narrator commits a truly frightening murder, leading his victim deep into the catacombs, chaining him there, and consigning him to a slow and solitary death. The murderer says that his purpose is to avenge a wrong that his victim has done him, but he does not reveal the nature of the wrong, and this omission leaves his readers searching for a motive. An understanding of this character is crucial to an understanding of the story, so it is necessary to study every comment for clues. The narrator speaks about his family and about social position. Certainly these are important themes in the tale.

Other themes are bound up in the setting. Death is obviously one of the story's themes, but the setting in the catacombs suggests associations with Christianity. Other religious imagery includes the drinking of wine and the ringing of bells. With Christianity comes the theme of resurrection as well as death, and also the themes of sin and atonement, judgment, salvation, and damnation.

Still other themes are best viewed in terms of the cultural milieu in which the tale appeared. Premature burial was an extremely popular topic in the mass media of Poe's time. Personal feuds, including well-known feuds involving Poe himself, also received media attention.

The tale may also be viewed allegorically or metaphorically, as a depiction of two sides of a single personality. The meanings of the two men's names mirror each other, as do their respective social positions. From a psychological perspective, Montresor's attack on Fortunato might be viewed as revealing deep sources of resentment or as representing an attempt or desire to bury a part of himself.

To see how the story might be read in several different ways, look at a paragraph near the end of the story. It is just before midnight, and Montresor is nearly finished building the wall that will enclose Fortunato.

> A succession of loud and shrill screams, bursting suddenly from the throat of the chained form, seemed to thrust me violently back. For a brief moment I hesitated—I trembled. Unsheathing my rapier, I began to grope with it about the recess: but the thought of an instant reassured me. I placed my hand upon the solid fabric of the catacombs, and felt satisfied. I reapproached the wall. I replied to the yells of him who clamored. I re-echoed—I aided—I surpassed them in volume and in strength. I did this, and the clamorer grew still.

In this passage, Fortunato screams, Montresor screams back, and Fortunato is silenced. That much is clear enough, but the paragraph also raises questions. Referring to the initial screams as coming from the "throat of the chained form" is peculiar, and the phrase "the yells of him who clamored" seems downright awkward. There is no doubt that the clamorer is Fortunato, yet why does the narrator not refer to him more plainly as "Fortunato" or "my friend," as he has all along? Perhaps this is a strategy to make him seem less human or less of an individual, so as to reduce in some way the horror of what Montresor is doing. Obscuring Fortunato's identity may also confuse or intertwine the identities of the two men. The action itself does that, since by the end of the passage it is Montresor who is screaming, while oxymoronically he "who clamored" is silent. Such merging or reversal of identity suggests a reading of the paragraph through an allegorical or psychological filter that interprets the characters as two sides of one self. From such a standpoint, what sort of mental activity is suggested by the image of one part of the mind "chaining" the other, walling it up, and shouting down its screams?

Other questions are raised by Montresor's fearful response to Fortunato's screams. What is the nature of Montresor's fear? Does he momentarily fear that someone will hear the screams and that his deed will be discovered? That interpretation is possible: His "thought of an instant" and his touching the "solid fabric" of the catacombs may be read as reassuring him that no one can possibly hear, and perhaps his own screaming is designed to demonstrate this assurance to Fortunato. But what is his purpose in poking his sword around in the darkness of the recess? What might this action represent? Does it suggest a different kind of fear?

The paragraph might also be read as emblematic of Montresor's feelings about what he is doing. Up to this point he has expressed nothing but assurance; he has been in complete control of his carefully planned revenge. Now he hesitates and trembles. Have his feelings changed as Fortunato's end comes nearer? Or were his previous remarks just bravado? Examine both his subsequent and his previous commentary to settle these questions.

In this brief and seemingly simple paragraph, then, are puzzling features that require you to approach remarks from different viewpoints. Ambiguities, omissions, and other peculiarities in the narrative invite and support a wide variety of interpretation. The questions the story raises have long been debated and may never be resolved. Some readers find this feature of the tale delightful, others find it frustrating, and still others feel both ways at once.

TOPICS AND STRATEGIES
Themes

Sometimes the theme of a story may be clearly stated, as the theme of revenge is in this tale. Yet the tale can be read in different ways, and a variety of themes can be identified. Montresor's references to Fortunato's rising fortunes as opposed to his own falling ones raise the theme of money and social position. References to religious rituals suggest themes such as guilt, sin, and redemption. Similarities between Montresor and Fortunato support a psychological reading, depicting a mind in conflict with itself.

In writing about any of these themes, collect details to formulate a specific idea. The topics listed below provide examples of how to narrow your focus and move from ideas in the story to what these ideas suggest about some aspect of the human condition.

Sample Topics:

1. **Revenge:** Revenge consists of retaliation against a person in response to a real or perceived injury or insult. Revenge is bound up with the concept of justice but also with baser human emotions such as spite, vindictiveness, and resentment. What do Montresor's words and actions suggest about the search for revenge?

   This topic offers several good avenues of approach. One is to consider the wellsprings of revenge. In this tale, revenge is no aberrant streak in Montresor's personality but a core value of his family, enshrined in the family's heraldic motto. What drives the thirst for revenge?

   Failing to exact revenge is unthinkable to Montresor, yet there may be signs that he is troubled by his actions. You might consider his frequent suggestions to Fortunato that they turn back, his frightened reaction to Fortunato's screams, and his words at the very end of the tale. In the last words, Montresor says, "May he rest in peace." Is this line ironic? To whom does it refer? Fifty years later, which man is at peace, and which is not? You might also consider Montresor's feelings as a Catholic, that is, a member of a religion that rejects the exaction of revenge. The tale's many references to religion are discussed further in the next question.

   An essay might also explore Montresor's attitudes toward revenge in relation to yours. To what extent do you empathize with Montresor, and to what extent do you judge him? What in his story and in his words inclines you to one reaction or the other? Most readers wonder what injury was done to him. Why does he withhold this information, and what effect does his withholding it have?

2. **Religion:** Religious references abound in the tale. What does the story suggest about religion and its role in life?

An essay on this topic should examine the pervasive presence of religious ideas and imagery. Montresor enacts a ritual burial, which features many of the trappings of church services, including the burning of candles, the ringing of bells, and the drinking of wine. The catacombs, too, are rich in religious associations. How are these elements related to Montresor's tale of revenge? Is the burial/murder a devotional act? Does it represent some kind of sacrifice? If so, to what sort of god? Or is the religious setting and ritual ironic or defiantly antireligious like a witches' black mass?

Some readers believe that the person Montresor is speaking to, 50 years after the murder, is a priest at confession. Is there evidence in the story that Montresor is troubled by his act and is seeking pardon and solace in his religion? If so, does he seem successful in the attempt?

3. **Masquerade:** How is the idea of masquerade used in the tale? What might the story be saying about masking and pretending?

Masquerade can be considered on several levels. On the most basic level, the masquerade and the liveliness of the carnival contrast with the deadly seriousness of Montresor's revenge. Other points of contrast might be noted, including the gaiety and spontaneity of the carnival and the sense of abandon. Carnival is a time when social restraints and the demands of the social order are often set aside.

Masquerading can also be viewed in terms of hiding one's identity and pretending to be what one is not. The story presents many ideas about issues of deception and the conflict between outward appearance and inner reality. Montresor vilifies Fortunato for practicing "imposture" on others for financial gain. Yet Montresor prides himself on his own imposture toward Fortunato. Indeed, he seems to take even greater satisfaction from his cleverness in fooling Fortunato than from his revenge itself. What could that be about?

Though masks conceal, may they not also reveal? What a man hides and what he pretends to be may tell much about his fears and aspirations. What do Montresor's black mask and Fortunato's motley reveal about them?

4. **Family:** Montresor speaks about his family and ancestry. How do they help shape his identity and his fate?

An essay taking this approach would collect the references to Montresor's heritage and form a picture of the family and its influence on him. How does its former greatness and present low estate affect his feelings and actions? How, too, might the family's decline be related to its single-minded code of honor? You might also consider what significance can be attached to the fact that this once "great and numerous" family now nearly all lie dead in the catacombs. And what is the significance of Fortunato's being buried alongside them?

As for Montresor himself, he expresses great pride in his heritage, but is he in some way trapped by his sense of past glory? Or by the family's unyielding demand for vengeance? Is the influence of the family a genuine source of strength for him, or does it lead him, against his nobler instincts, to his own destruction?

5. **The divided self:** How might the tale be seen as a depiction of psychological doubles, or two sides of a personality at war with each other?

For a story to create psychological doubles, it must find ways to link the characters while highlighting the differences between them. An essay on this topic might begin by noting the characteristics that Montresor and Fortunato share, as well as the narrative devices that tend to fuse the two men. The essay could then describe the differences between the men and suggest how these differences might represent different aspects of the human mind or self. Does Fortunato represent a more carefree, less repressive spirit? Or should the contrast be viewed more in terms of success and power? You might go on to interpret the action of the tale in terms of this conflict. In

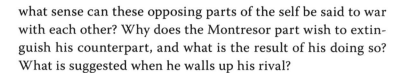

what sense can these opposing parts of the self be said to war with each other? Why does the Montresor part wish to extinguish his counterpart, and what is the result of his doing so? What is suggested when he walls up his rival?

Character

The story focuses on two characters, and readers are provided with somewhat more personal information on them than in many Poe stories. Montresor lives in a palazzo beneath which lie extensive catacombs. He is of the nobility and was at one time rich and respected. Fortunato appears to be newly wealthy and a freemason. They share a knowledge of wine. Is is not revealed, however, what the cause of the reversal of Montresor's fortunes was or what has caused him to seek revenge against Fortunato. The omission of this seemingly basic information strongly colors a reading of the tale.

Sample Topics:

1. **Montresor's resentment:** Discuss the nature and sources of Montresor's thirst for revenge.

   Montresor's stated motive is retribution for some wrong that Fortunato has done him, but he never mentions the nature of this injury. What signs are there that his resentment is deeper and more general? Does he dislike Fortunato as a person? Does he resent Fortunato's position? To what extent and in what ways is Montresor moved by feelings about his family? Might his revenge against Fortunato represent an attempt to live up to family tradition or to reclaim a family glory that has been lost?

2. **Montresor's attitude toward his crime:** Through most of the tale, Montresor appears to enjoy the revenge he exacts on Fortunato, but the ending of the tale gives many readers the opposite feeling. Discuss how Montresor feels about what he has done.

   Before writing on this topic, weigh the evidence on both sides. Consider the delight Montresor expresses in telling how he duped his victim, as well as the terror he exhibits at the end. Is he truly ambivalent? Or is one side a mask? Perhaps he affects glee in order to hide a deeper compunction? Or does the relish he takes in outwitting Fortunato reflect his deepest feelings, whereas his somber demeanor at the conclusion amounts to no more than a nod to conventional morality?

It might be useful in this connection to consider the frame of the story. To whom might Montresor be speaking, and what is his purpose in telling this tale? The only evidence is the tale itself: Does it seem as if he is seeking sympathy and forgiveness from his listener or admiration? Your answer can only be speculative. Choose a position and provide reasons—based on details from the story—to support it.

3. **Fortunato's folly:** Describe the character of Fortunato. In what sense is he responsible for his own death?

Montresor offers numerous unflattering opinions of Fortunato's character, but you should rely primarily on the evidence of the victim's own words and actions. In what ways does Montresor play upon Fortunato's pride? Does the ease with which Fortunato is tricked reveal him as simple and trustful or complacent and self-involved? Does his pride, which ultimately proves fatal to him, seem more like a grievous fault or a mere foible? What indications are there of his attitudes toward Montresor, and how do these add to your picture of his character?

History and Context

Certain elements of "The Cask of Amontillado" seem to connect directly to issues in Poe's life. Some believe that Poe was drawing on a feud he had with one of his literary rivals. Others see in Montresor's family history strong echoes of Poe's own fall from wealth to poverty. Essays that provide biographical or sociohistorical context often make stimulating reading, but they must be carefully crafted. An essay should provide ample information but must also connect the contextual information with elements in the tale itself. At the same time, you should avoid making too absolute a claim about the connection between real events and events in the story.

Sample Topics:

1. **Poe's feud with Thomas Dunn English:** In what ways can the tale be read in relation to the literary feud between Poe and Thomas Dunn English?

   Poe and English savaged and satirized each other's work in a series of articles and at one point even engaged in a fistfight on a New York street. The appearance of "The Cask of Amontillado" at this time invites the speculation that Poe may have had this feud in mind. To write an essay on this topic, research the feud and read the articles by the two men. You might discover striking specific parallels between the articles and Poe's story. Certainly, you should be able to make general connections between the feelings and concerns exhibited in the articles and those reflected in the tale. When all is said and done, your essay should probably portray Poe less as recording or extending his feud than as turning his experience into a work of literature that captures both the intensity and the complexity of the human thirst for revenge.

2. **Poe's resentment toward his foster father, John Allan:** How might Montresor's feelings about his and Fortunato's social position reflect similar attitudes expressed by Poe?

   The decline in the fortunes of the Montresors strikingly resembles Poe's own fortunes in life. Taken into a wealthy family at age three, Poe grew up with a level of material comfort that he lost as an adult, when John Allan cut off his support. Poe's resentment is manifest in many of his letters to and about Allan and also, it can be argued, in his attitudes toward and dealings with people in comfortable circumstances. You could consult biographies of Poe as well as a collection of Poe's letters for material that would be relevant in relation to Montresor's resentments and animosities over wealth and social standing.

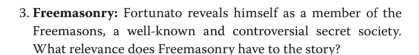

3. **Freemasonry:** Fortunato reveals himself as a member of the
   Freemasons, a well-known and controversial secret society.
   What relevance does Freemasonry have to the story?

   The reference to Freemasonry is brief and involves a joke: Fortunato asks Montresor for a sign that he is a Mason, and Montresor
   shows him the brickmason's trowel with which he intends to wall
   Fortunato up. An essay would draw on research about the nature
   and history of Freemasonry and suggest what role the topic plays
   in relation to the tale as a whole. You might, for example, note the
   conflict that existed at one time between Freemasons and Catho-
   lics. How might this conflict be related to Montresor's animosity
   toward Fortunato? How does this religious conflict connect to
   other references to religion in the tale?

4. **Premature burial:** What ideas about premature burial were
   common in Poe's time, and how might they affect your reading
   of the tale?

   Live burial was at one time a practiced form of capital punishment
   for certain offenses. In addition, the fear of being buried alive was
   a common terror in Poe's time, fueled by actual cases and sensational media attention. Poe himself published several articles on
   the topic. A key question for readers of "The Cask of Amontillado"
   is why Montresor chooses this method of killing his adversary.
   Another avenue of approach is to ask what sorts of fears or associations are activated in readers by this particular punishment.
   Published research on the subject of premature burial is plentiful
   and could provide interesting ideas for either approach.

Form and Genre

Several formal aspects of the tale offer particular interest. One is the
narrative frame. In a sense, "The Cask of Amontillado" is not the story of
a man who kills another but that of a man who tells about something he
did long ago. This frame turns the focus, at least in part, from the event
itself to how Montresor feels about the event, and how he represents it,
some 50 years later.

The tale is suffused with irony of different types or layers. Montresor is deliberately ironic when he offers a toast to Fortunato's long life and when he urges Fortunato once more to leave the catacombs after he has shackled him. A deeper irony emerges when Montresor's remarks cause us to reflect on Montresor himself. In telling his story, he seems to assume that his listener will enjoy his mocking of his victim, but readers' true reactions are far more mixed.

Sample Topics:

1. **Narrative frame:** The tale is the record of a man speaking or writing 50 years after the events in question. How does this narrative frame color your reading of the story?

The frame of the tale invites conjecture as to the circumstances of its telling. To whom is Montresor telling his story, and for what purpose? The tale offers only the scantest of clues. The long lapse of time invites speculation on how his memory of the deed has affected him, as well as what the circumstances of his life have been. Probe for clues in the way that he speaks of these happenings. What tone or attitude does he adopt? Is it consistent? If you speculate on who his listener may be, you may at the same time try to imagine the listener's reactions. What reactions does Montresor seem to want to elicit? Do some of his remarks undercut the posture he intends to project? Finally, an essay could discuss the very process of speculation. What effect does your asking these questions, which may have no conclusive answers, have on your attitudes toward this character, his actions, and Poe's tale?

2. **Irony:** Discuss Poe's use of irony in the story.

Irony, in which statements convey meanings at variance with their apparent or intended meanings, pervades this tale. Some derives from Montresor's duplicity, his pose as Fortunato's friend. Montresor's expressed concern for Fortunato's health and his toast to his companion's long life fall into this category. Other examples seem to have deeper roots. How do you interpret the final sentence: *"In pace requiescat!"*? Is this a sincere prayer over a now-vanquished rival, or is it a taunt? For some readers, the real irony of the words is that the prayer is more aptly offered to Montresor than Fortunato.

An effective essay would consider what the irony adds to the story. Does Montresor's taunting irony reveal his character? Does the irony, in which meanings themselves are disguised, complement the story's theme of masquerade? It might be argued that the pervasiveness of remarks that can be taken in different ways contributes to the generalized feeling of uncertainty that many readers of the tale experience.

3. **Setting:** Discuss the setting of the story and its relation to the tale as a whole.

This topic may be approached from any of several directions. On an emotional level, the catacombs contribute to the horror that the tale elicits. In addition, the catacombs by their nature and history contribute to the themes of death, resurrection, religious ritual, and religious persecution. Besides noting connections between the tale and general ideas about the catacombs, an essay should examine how the text creates associations of its own by the specific ways in which the setting is described. In what ways, for example, does the fact that these are the Montresors' private family vaults interact with themes of family and tradition?

Compare and Contrast Essays

The goal of any literary essay is to show insight into the work being discussed. Compare and contrast essays that merely catalog a succession of similarities and differences often fail to show much insight. It is usually preferable to focus on one or a very few key points of similarity or difference that can be discussed in some relation to the work as a whole. One strategy is to try to complete a sentence such as the following: "This similarity (or difference) is important (or noteworthy or interesting) because. . . ." If you can complete this sentence meaningfully, you are on your way to an effective essay.

Sample Topics:

1. **Comparing Montresor and Fortunato:** The two men have certain similarities, while in other respects they seem almost opposite. Discuss these similarities and differences in the context of the story.

   Going beyond merely enumerating similarities and differences, an essay should identify a pattern of characteristics or focus on the most relevant ones. Might the characters be considered mirror images of each other? What is gained by viewing them in this way? In making these comparisons, bear in mind that your sole source of information is Montresor, a man who is eager to point out the faults of his rival while minimizing his own and who may wish to emphasize the differences between him and his adversary.

2. **Comparing "The Cask of Amontillado" to "William Wilson":** Both tales depict rivalries that end in murder. Consider other similarities between the tales, as well as the differences, and discuss them in terms of the overall effects of the two works.

   There are many points of comparison. Both tales can be seen as portraying doubles, both involve masquerades, both raise issues of social standing and class resentment, the labyrinthine halls of William Wilson's school bear a striking similarity to the catacombs, and both tales are told in the first person by the murdering rival. What do such similarities suggest, about either Poe's preoccupations or his methods in constructing his fiction? Do these similarities underpin broader similarities between the two tales in theme or style? At the same time, what are the differences within the similarities? In what ways, for example, are the masquerades handled differently in the two works? How do these differences reflect different aims in the two tales or create different effects for the reader?

Bibliography for "The Cask of Amontillado"

Bondensen, Jan. *Buried Alive: The Terrifying History of our Most Primal Fear.* New York: W. W. Norton & Co., 2001.

Claudy, Carl H. *Introduction to Freemasonry.* Morristown, NJ: Temple Books, 1959.

Delaney, Bill. "Poe's 'The Cask of Amontillado.'" *Explicator* 64 (2005): 39–41.

Gruesser, John. "Poe's 'The Cask of Amontillado.'" *Explicator* 56 (1998): 129.

Hodapp, Christopher. *Freemasons for Dummies.* Hoboken, NJ: Wiley Publishing, 2005.

Hoffman, Daniel. "Murder." *Poe Poe Poe Poe Poe Poe Poe.* New York: Doubleday, 1972. 218–26.

Poe, Edgar Allan. *Essay and Reviews.* Notes by G. R. Thompson. New York: Library of America, 1984.

———. *The Letters of Edgar Allan Poe.* Ed. John Ward Ostrom. 2 vols. Cambridge, MA: Harvard UP, 1948.

Quinn, Arthur Hobson. "Widening Horizons—Friends and Enemies." *Edgar Allan Poe.* 1941. Reprint, with a foreword by Shawn Rosenheim, Baltimore: Johns Hopkins UP, 1998. 496–534.

Reynolds, David. "Temperance Literature." *Beneath the American Renaissance.* Cambridge, MA: Harvard UP, 1988. 65–73.

St. John Stott, Graham. "Poe's 'The Cask of Amontillado.'" *Explicator* 62 (2004): 85–88.

Silverman, Kenneth. *Edgar A. Poe: Mournful and Never-Ending Remembrance.* New York: HarperCollins, 1991.

THE NARRATIVE OF ARTHUR GORDON PYM

READING TO WRITE

*T*HE *NARRATIVE* of *Arthur Gordon Pym* tells the story of a young man's journey from innocence to experience. His odyssey may be seen as a rite of passage, but what is the nature of his experience, and where does his journey lead him? Does the novel trace a progression toward spirituality and authentic selfhood or a blind movement toward an abyss of meaninglessness?

Pym's tale is dramatic but at every level enigmatic. Dreams and hallucinations mingle with stated events. The events themselves range from the incredible to the outlandish and beyond. Furthermore, the narrative is framed by introductory and concluding notes that explicitly and humorously call into question the veracity and even the authorship of the account. As if to make the puzzle complete, the ending of the story is omitted.

The novel offers adventure, madness, secret writing, the discovery of a new world, and more, thus lending itself to a wide array of readings. In general, critical analyses may be grouped into two broad perspectives: one that tends to see Pym's voyage as a journey toward enlightenment and redemption and one that views the novel as a study in the deceptive and the inscrutable.

Two passages from the novel illustrate these alternative readings. The first appears in chapter 2, when Pym is hiding in the hold of the *Grampus*:

> I fell, in spite of every exertion to the contrary, into a state of profound sleep, or rather stupor. My dreams were of the most terrific description. Every species of calamity and horror befell me. Among other miseries, I was smothered to death between huge pillows, by demons of the most ghastly and ferocious aspect. Immense serpents held me in their embrace, and looked earnestly in my face with their fearful shining eyes. Ten deserts, limitless, and of the most forlorn and awe-inspiring character, spread themselves out before me. Immensely tall trunks of trees, gray and leafless, rose up in endless succession as far as the eye could reach. Their roots were concealed in wide-spreading morasses, whose dreary water lay intensely black, still, and altogether terrible, beneath. And the strange trees seemed endowed with human vitality, and waving to and fro their skeleton arms, were crying to the silent waters for mercy, in the shrill and piercing accents of the most acute agony and despair. The scene changed; and I stood, naked and alone, amid the burning sand-plains of Zahara.

One way to read this passage is to analyze the dream imagery for metaphorical meanings. On such a reading, the dream offers a fairly straightforward image of death and rebirth. Pym sees himself smothered to death, sinking into a black marsh, and finally awakening, naked, in a new land. Examining the details of the dream, you might interpret the demons as representing evil in the world, while the serpent calls to mind the story of Eden and the Fall of Man from innocence to guilty knowledge. If you attempt to relate this dream to the rest of the novel, there are almost limitless connections. The dream occurs in the ship's hold, where Pym is boxed up and in a sense undersea, so that he may be viewed as simultaneously in a tomb and in a womb. Just previously Augustus has described him as buried for three days—like Jesus before his resurrection. Expanding outward from this scene, the death-rebirth pattern repeats itself throughout the novel. The tale is essentially structured as a recurring cycle of episodes in which Pym comes near to death and then is miraculously saved.

While the meaning of the dream may be straightforwardly analyzed, the context in which it is presented gives rise to objections. One is the peculiar passage of time. Previously Pym has slept, and when he awakes it appears that many days had passed—enough for his meat to completely putrefy. It seems impossible under normal circumstances that he could have slept so long. Is he dreaming about the meat when he thinks he is awake? Is he in some state other than normal sleep? By setting us this puzzle, the passage casts itself as something other than the straightforward presentation of Pym's dream. Moreover, the circumstances under which he wakes from the dream call into question the seriousness of the entire episode. He wakes to find a beast standing over him. Petrified, he resigns himself to die, only to see his own dog jump on him and start licking his face, giving him "an overpowering sense of deliverance and reanimation." A moment before, the novel has provided a deep and symbolic description, evoking, in the most poetic terms, the timeless literary theme of death and rebirth. Now it reduces the image to that of a dog licking his owner's face. How seriously, we may well wonder, should this story be taken?

The second passage comes at the end of the novel, just before the concluding note.

> March 22. The darkness had materially increased, relieved only by the glare of the water thrown back from the white curtain before us. Many gigantic and pallidly white birds flew continuously now from beyond the veil, and their scream was the eternal *Tekeli-li!* As they retreated from our vision. Hereupon Nu-Nu stirred in the bottom of the boat; but upon touching him, we found his spirit departed. And now we rushed into the embraces of the cataract, where a chasm threw itself open to receive us. But there arose in our pathway a shrouded human figure, very far larger in its proportions than any dweller among men. And the hue of the skin of the figure was of the perfect whiteness of the snow.

This passage presents a similar choice in interpretation. On the one hand, it fits perfectly with the death-rebirth motif observed above. While the passage seems to suggest annihilation, its use of words and phrases such as "eternal," "embraces," and "threw itself open to receive us" implies something far more benign. As Pym moves toward the warm white water and the womblike vortex, he may be viewed, once more, as moving toward rebirth, toward not the mere extinction of the consciousness but the realization of a superconsciousness in the moment of the self's annihilation.

Such an interpretation, however, is at the very least open to question, for the conclusion could not be more inconclusive. Like the impenetrable whiteness into which Pym sails, his fate and the meaning of his journey remain uncertain. This is particularly so because the ending of the novel is missing—and missing under the most dubious of circumstances. The introductory and concluding notes show that Pym survived this encounter and returned to tell the entire story. The last chapters are missing, it is said, because of Pym's accidental death, and it is suggested that the editor (Poe himself) refuses to provide them. All efforts to understand the novel are thus deliberately blocked by its author. All of this editorial humbug, which is quite humorous, suggests to many that the tale is concerned less with the personal or spiritual growth of a young man than with the uncertainty of tales and the chicanery of their tellers.

TOPICS AND STRATEGIES
Themes

If you are given a choice of themes to write about, you would do well to reflect on how the novel speaks to you. Does it feel like a genuine journey of the mind or spirit, even if defining that journey seems difficult? Is your primary experience instead one of confusion or bewilderment? Or do you feel most inclined to laugh, or at least smile, at the novel's bizarre twists and turns? Starting with your feelings about the book, try to identify what specifically gives rise to those feelings. It should then be possible for you to relate this material to at least one of the themes discussed below. If you find true growth or progression in the story, you will probably lean toward the second or third option. The enigmatic quality of the novel is explored in the first and fourth option. Interpretations involving humor or hoaxing can be explored in the first and second option.

Sample Topics:

1. **Deception:** At every level and from virtually every perspective, things in the novel are not what they appear to be. What roles do obfuscation and deception play in the story?

   Essays may approach this theme from many directions. On the one hand, Pym is continually deceived about the true nature of events. He also is repeatedly the victim of deliberate deceit. Is his misreading of situations the result of some blindness in himself or the inevitable consequence of uncertain existence? On the other hand, Pym is himself a deceiver, creating disguises, false stories, ruses, and various concealments. Is deceit a universal attribute? Or is Pym's deception somehow different from that of other characters? Are there levels, then, of deceit?

Pym constantly tries to make sense of his experience and constantly is confounded in the attempt. Does the novel suggest that fundamentally what deceives us is the belief that the world is meaningful?

Are we similarly deceived about literature? The usual assumption is that at some level, in some way, books make sense. Yet *Pym* itself is a deception. An essay might examine the introductory note, which explicitly calls into question both the "truthfulness" of the narrative and even the identity of its author. What is the nature of the deceit involved in presenting the story as true when it is not? What ideas about the meaningfulness of literature are implied by a novel whose ending is missing or even deliberately withheld, making it impossible to reach a conclusion about its meaning?

2. **Death/rebirth:** From his initial brush with death on the *Ariel* to his final trip through the veil of whiteness, Pym repeatedly faces extinction only to arise again. What ideas does the novel suggest about human renewal?

This topic is discussed in the "Reading to Write" section. References to and images of death and birth abound in the story, making it a simple matter to establish the presence of this theme in the novel. But what ideas does the book present about rebirth? In literature rebirth typically represents some kind of renewal: the power of the human spirit to rebound from adversity, or the ability of a character to overcome his sin or weakness, or in religious terms, resurrection and eternal life. An essay could collect evidence pointing to any of these ideas in order to flesh out a theory of what *Pym* is suggesting about rebirth.

Alternatively, you could collect evidence that the book actually means to undercut the apparent message of renewal.

The "Reading to Write" section considers whether the image of Pym's dog licking his face trivializes the idea of rebirth. In a similar vein, do Pym's miraculous deliverances grow so preposterous as to suggest that the book is poking fun at its own theme?

3. **Identity/the divided self:** What ideas does the novel raise about the struggle of the mind to create a stable ego structure?

It is possible to view Pym's voyage as depicting a psychological journey. To write from this perspective, think of Pym's experiences metaphorically. Consider, as an example, how you might interpret the early scenes that take place in the hold of the *Grampus.* What psychological ideas are suggested by the labyrinth of barrels and crates, his confinement, his dreams, his fears of death, and the unreadable message he receives? Pym seems to jump from one location and one bizarre experience to another. Could the different ships and experiences represent different mental states? What is the nature of these states? Does the succession of states suggest any pattern?

You might argue that Pym's journey represents a search for identity. In the story, Pym seems to share identities, first with Augustus and later with Dirk Peters. Might these characters represent aspects of human nature? What psychological process, in that case, might Pym's shifting identities represent?

4. **Secret writing:** Pym encounters several texts that he is unable to comprehend. What does the novel say about writing and the search for meaning?

First, you could examine the explicit references to texts: the indecipherable note that Pym receives from Augustus, the hieroglyphics in the caves of Tsalal, and perhaps the chasms themselves, which are drawn like letters or characters in a written language. What is the nature of Pym's encounters with text? What is the outcome? What do these episodes suggest about human attempts to understand text? Next, you might consider the book as a whole. How does your experience of the novel—your attempt to understand it—parallel Pym's experience of the texts he encounters?

Character

An important issue in the discussion of character is individuality. Some fictional characters have unforgettable individual personalities. Other characters are less particularly drawn. This is often the case in adventure stories, which are more interested in action than personality. Pym's behavior mainly consists of immediate reactions to the situations he encounters. He seems to react the way anyone would in such circumstances and so does not emerge as a unique individual.

Still other characters represent types. The ruthless villain, the kindly old neighbor, the spoiled heiress—such characters are drawn specifically enough that they can be identified as the sort of people they are, but not so specifically that they can be known as individuals. Minor characters are often drawn in this manner, but when major characters appear as types, the story does not seem to be mainly interested in individual personalities. In some cases, the characters may represent ideas, and their interaction can be read in terms of those ideas. In *Pym*, for example, many readers believe that Dirk Peters represents natural man and Augustus Barnard civilized man.

It is important, then, to think about characters in the context of the works in which they appear. When characters lack individuality, as they do in *Pym*, this may be part of the design of the book.

Sample Topics:

1. **Dirk Peters as noble savage:** The "noble savage" embodies the concept of a human being untainted by the corrupting influences of civilization. How does Dirk Peters exemplify this concept?

   To discuss the character in these terms, you might first describe his physical attributes and parentage. How do these suggest a primitive nature? Next you could review his behavior in the tale. What behavior marks him as raw or unsophisticated? At the same time, what virtues does he exhibit? Could these be described as natural virtues? How do you interpret the fact that Peters repeatedly saves Pym from death? How do you interpret the concluding image of Peters and Pym sailing into the abyss together?

2. **Augustus's character:** How is Augustus Barnard depicted in the novel, and what ideas are suggested by his behavior and his fate?

If Peters may be viewed as uncivilized, to what extent is Augustus a product of civil society? Consider his family background, his education, and his behavior, particularly his interaction with Pym. Immersed in language, Augustus tells sea stories that entrance Pym and draw Pym to him. But how helpful is he to Pym? His written message proves useless to Pym, and on more than one occasion his sophistication turns to trickery. Finally, what is suggested by his inability to survive on the open sea?

3. **Pym's search for identity:** In what ways is Pym depicted as a young man seeking to discover his place in the world?

An essay on this topic would focus on characteristics of Pym that are typical of young adults. How do his motivations in undertaking his journey suggest youthful curiosity and adventurousness? How do his fears and insecurities, often revealed by his dreams or hallucinations, reflect common anxieties of youth? From here you should probably explore how his experiences could be viewed as shaping his growth to manhood. Finally, how do you interpret, from this perspective, the conclusion of the story?

Pym's passivity is also worthy of attention, either in relation to the view of him as a young man in search of himself or as a topic in itself. After initially deciding to go to sea, Pym does little to assert his own goals or personality. He seems not to act but to react to the calamities that befall him. Why does the novel depict him in this way? Is he a dupe? Is he a survivor, in the sense of someone with the strength to carry on in the face of adversity? Is he a kind of everyman, or pilgrim seeking his personal destiny?

History and Context

Many contextual connections may be made between racial conflict in *Pym* and race relations in Poe's America. Writing about race, however, requires sensitivity as well as awareness of the complexity of cultural comparisons. On the one hand, the racism that pervaded antebellum America, as well as the condescension of whites to both black Americans and aboriginal peoples, is repugnant to today's consciousness. But merely condemning these attitudes is not useful. Nor is it useful to point out the obvious racism in *Pym* and condemn Poe for his hateful attitudes. On the other hand, it is similarly inappropriate to observe that white attitudes of racial superiority were common in Poe's time and that he merely reflected the culture he came from. An essay can avoid these common failings by focusing on specific connections between Poe's text and particular currents in the racial tensions of his day.

Sample Topics:

1. **Race:** Discuss racial themes in *Pym* in the context of the racial tensions of antebellum America.

In 1831 Nat Turner led a slave rebellion in Virginia that brought about the slaughter of 55 white men, women, and children. Turner's and other slave uprisings crystallized whites' fear of rebellion and retribution at the hands of black slaves, a fear that bred widespread belief in black savagery.

Conflict between blacks and whites is quite explicit in the novel, most notably in the person of the black mutineer Seymour and the encounter with the inhabitants of Tsalal. The sailors of the *Jane Guy* dismiss these natives as "ignorant savages," and Pym describes them as "among the most barbarous, subtle, and blood-thirsty wretches that ever contaminated the face of the globe." What irony is involved in reading these words by a man who himself has engaged in cannibalism? What signs are there of the sources of the sailors' prejudice? Also, what are the consequences of their racism? Does their ignorant dismissal of the natives contribute to their failure to understand the local taboo about whiteness?

2. **Polar expeditions:** Polar exploration was a matter of broad contemporary interest in Poe's time, receiving wide coverage in newspapers and magazines, including the one that Poe edited. What ideas about polar exploration does the novel suggest or exploit?

In researching polar expeditions, it would be valuable to see how they were regarded in Poe's time. Did they reflect the optimism and adventurousness of a growing nation? A desire to avoid confronting the serious social problems brought on by slavery and the ravages of the Industrial Revolution? Or both? Does Poe's tale seem to mirror one or the other of these viewpoints, or does it show both sides at once? Similar questions may be asked in terms of the science behind polar exploration, which was bound up with the popular theory that the earth was hollow and habitable and that the center was accessible through holes at the earth's poles. Does the hollow-earth theory, in the context of Poe's time, represent the expanding possibilities being opened by advances in science or the foolish readiness of the public to believe almost anything? How are either or both of these perspectives reflected in the novel?

Form and Genre

The narrative structure of the novel is complex and curious. Study the introductory and concluding notes carefully, first in order to understand what is being claimed about the truth and authorship of the book. From there, ponder the effects or purposes of these narrative frames.

What effect is created when Pym says that the tale is true though admittedly difficult to believe, when he says that Poe believed the story but suggested presenting it as fiction anyway, and when the writer of the concluding note says that Poe refused to believe any of the endings of the tale? Is the novel really pretending to be factual, or is it pretending to pretend to be factual? How does any of this incline you to read the story differently than you would if it were more straightforwardly presented?

It will help for you to acquaint yourself with the concept of metafiction. This term refers to self-referential writing that points to its own fictional devices in order to raise questions about the nature of writing, the status of literature as a thing in itself, and its relation to reality. Another concept to consider is parody, which pokes fun at certain writings or types of writing by imitating them and exaggerating their features. Finally, you might consider the hoax. A hoax is often thought of as an attempt to convince readers that a piece of writing is true when it is not, but there may be another form of hoaxing that brings readers in on the joke. Again, the nature and purposes of such hoaxing are curious matters that may be viewed in many different ways.

Sample Topics:

1. **The narrative frames:** Describe the narrative frames that precede and follow the story and discuss how they affect your reading of the novel.

   As discussed above, the story's unusual frames invite a variety of interpretations. A good strategy for an essay would be to identify one way in which the frames affect your reading of the novel. Do the references to the story's unbelievability, for example, cause you to reflect on the way that readers make believe when they approach a work of fiction? Does the confusion over who wrote the story and what happened to the lost ending extend the novel's theme of the inexplicable or the unreadable? Does the silliness of the claim that the story is true and that it was written not by Poe but by Pym encourage you to view the entire novel in a humorous light?

2. **Episodic structure:** The novel consists of a series of distinct episodes, each involving shipwreck, near-death, and rescue. Discuss this cyclical structure in terms of the overall design and themes of the novel.

   After describing the basic cycle, an essay could go on to discuss the sequence of cycles. Do they progress in some definable way or merely recapitulate each other? Is the conclusion an appropriately culminating event or merely one more in an endless series? Translating the structure into theme, does the pattern suggest that life involves a kind of growth to a higher level of development, or is life just an inescapable cycle of calamities without an ultimate meaning or end?

Compare and Contrast Essays

Comparing *Pym* with a more representative, less peculiar adventure story opens another window on the novel. Curiously, *Pym* can appear more serious, profound, and metaphysical than an ordinary sea story, or it can appear more ridiculous. In either case, the comparison enables you to explore just what makes Poe's novel so peculiar.

Sample Topics:

1. **Comparing adventure tales:** Compare one or more aspects of *Pym* with similar features in another adventure story or novel.

   An essay on this topic must first identify a specific point or points of comparison. You might compare sailing adventures in terms of their depiction of shipboard life, of interaction with native peoples, or of events such as mutiny, shipwreck, or cannibalism. There is no shortage of contemporary sailing adventures to choose from, including most famously Richard Henry Dana's *Two Years before the Mast* and Herman Melville's novels. (An ambitious paper could compare the image of whiteness in *Pym* and Melville's *Moby Dick*.) Jules Verne wrote a sequel to *Pym* called *The Sphinx of the Ice Fields*, in which a crew sets sail for the South Pole to try to learn what happened to Pym. Verne's sea tale *20,000 Leagues under the Sea* and his hollow-earth adventure *Journey to the Center of the Earth* might also be used for comparison.

2. **Comparing Augustus and Dirk Peters:** The contrast between these men might be considered a central feature of the novel. How would you describe the difference in their characters, and in what way is the contrast significant?

The depiction of these two men is discussed in the section on character. How might these men be viewed as representing either two sides of the human personality or two sides of human society? To what extent do their respective backgrounds and behavior mark one as representing nature and the other civilization? How do the characters compare in terms of their accomplishments, strength, moral character, and effect on Pym? What, then, is the novel suggesting about the wellsprings of human virtue?

Bibliography for *The Narrative of Arthur Gordon Pym*

Goddu, Teresa. *Gothic America*. New York: Columbia UP, 1993.

Harvey, Ronald C. *The Critical History of Edgar Allan Poe's* The Narrative of Arthur Gordon Pym. Oxford: Routledge, 1998.

Irwin, John T. *American Hieroglyphics: The Symbol of the Egyptian Hieroglyphics in the American Renaissance*. Baltimore: Johns Hopkins UP, 1980.

Jenkins, John S. *Explorations and Adventures in and about the Pacific and Antarctic Oceans: Voyage of the U.S. Exploring Squadron, 1838–1842*. New York: Butler Brothers, 1889.

Kennedy, J. Gerald. *Poe, Death, and the Life of Writing*. New Haven, CT: Yale UP, 1987.

———. "'Trust No Man': Poe, Douglass, and the Culture of Slavery." *Romancing the Shadow: Poe and Race*. Ed. J. Gerald Kennedy and Liliane Weissberg. New York: Oxford UP, 2001. 225–57.

Kopley, Richard, ed. *Poe's Pym: Critical Explorations*. Durham, NC: Duke UP, 1992.

Morrell, Benjamin. *A Narrative of Four Voyages: The South Sea, North and South Pacific Ocean, Chinese Sea, Ethiopic and Southern Atlantic Ocean, Indian and Antarctic Ocean from the Year 1822 to 1831*. Kessinger Publishing, 2005.

Philbrick, Nathaniel. *Sea of Glory: America's Voyage of Discovery, The U.S. Exploring Expedition, 1838–1842*. Madison, WI: Turtleback Books, 2004.

Standish, David. *Hollow Earth*. Cambridge, MA: Da Capo Press, 2006.

"THE RAVEN"

READING TO WRITE

"T HE RAVEN," which appeared in 1845, was an immediate sensation both in the United States and abroad, and today it stands as one of the most popular poems of all time. It added considerably to Poe's fame but brought him little money, for it was reprinted widely without permission.

"The Raven" is quintessential Poe. It takes up his favorite themes of loss and remembrance, mixes horror with whimsy, and relies heavily on astonishing, spellbinding rhythm and rhyme. The poem also typifies Poe in tracing the psychological breakdown of its narrator. A good way to write about the poem is to examine how it dramatizes this breakdown in terms of the speaker's changing behavior and statements and through the poem's diction, meter, and rhyme.

The first half of "The Raven" begins relatively calmly:

> Once upon a midnight dreary, while I pondered, weak and
> weary,
> Over many a quaint and curious volume of forgotten lore—
> While I nodded, nearly napping, suddenly there came a
> tapping,
> As of some one gently rapping, rapping at my chamber door—
> "'Tis some visiter," I muttered, "tapping at my chamber door—
> Only this and nothing more."

Though mourning his lost love, the speaker is reasonable. Healthily, he seeks "surcease of sorrow" (11). He also recognizes that the bird's apt replies to his first few comments are a matter of mere coincidence, that "Nevermore" is probably the only word the bird knows. But darker thoughts gradually take control of him.

By stanza 15 the narrator's mental state has greatly deteriorated:

> "Prophet!" said I, "thing of evil!—prophet still, if bird or
>   devil!—
> Whether Tempter sent, or whether tempest tossed thee
>   here ashore,
> Desolate yet all undaunted, on this desert land enchanted—
> On this home by Horror haunted—tell me truly, I implore—
> Is there—*is* there balm in Gilead?—tell me—tell me, I
>   implore!"
> Quoth the Raven "Nevermore."

These lines suggest loss of self-control, if not sanity, in several ways. At the level of the story, the speaker has worked himself into anger toward the bird. He considers it an evil prophet and is now asking it questions and expecting intelligent answers. He crafts his question, of course, knowing what the bird will say. This being the case, his question whether there is balm in Gilead implies that he has now given up his hope for surcease of sorrow. A similar analysis could be applied to the intervening and succeeding stanzas.

The speaker's increasing agitation can also be traced in his loss of verbal control. In the last three lines of the stanza above, he is practically sputtering. There is also a cumulative effect from the incessant rhyme scheme. The repetition in every stanza of the same "-ore" rhyme grows obsessive. In addition, there is almost too much rhyme: internal rhymes in the first and third lines of each stanza and the rhyme in the third line repeated in the middle of the fourth. This rhyme scheme is consistent throughout the poem, but with each repetition it feels more manic.

The foregoing discussion limns the basic movement in the poem from hope to despair. Within this framework, the poem offers much of interest. Different readers will be drawn to different motifs and features of the poem.

TOPICS AND STRATEGIES
Themes

"Beauty," wrote Poe, "is the sole legitimate province of the poem." Further, "Melancholy is . . . the most legitimate of all the poetical tones." "The Raven" clearly embodies Poe's favorite themes of beauty, love, loss, and sadness. In writing about theme in poetry, however, you should not merely describe what the poem says, but how it says it. How do the elements of diction, meter, and rhyme—and changes in these elements—suggest ideas about the theme?

Sample Topics:

1. **Loss:** How does "The Raven" confront the idea of loss?

   The speaker laments the loss of a loved one. Obviously, the poem expresses the mourner's pain, but how is the experience reflected in the poem's construction? How do the speaker's thoughts progress from beginning to end? How are these changes reflected by changes in the poem's diction and style?

2. **Madness:** As discussed in the "Reading to Write" section, "The Raven" traces the descent of a man from sorrow to hopelessness or even madness. What ideas do the poems suggest about the path of this descent?

   An essay could attempt to identify stages in the narrator's descent. What behavior typifies the different stages? How do changes in the man's questions reflect a deepening despair? Also, what role does the pattern of rhythm and rhyme play?

3. **Dreams:** How might the poem represent dreaming?

   The initial setting may suggest to readers that the poem is describing a dream. In what ways do you experience the poem differently if you read it as a dream? Does dreaming provide escape, release, solace, or healing, as is sometimes thought, or does it further agitate the troubled mind?

Language, Symbols, and Imagery

It seems impossible to underestimate the role that is played in the poem by its hypnotic sound. An essay should explain not only how Poe creates the sounds of the poem but also the purposes for which he uses them.

As haunting as the poem's sound is its unforgettable image of the raven. Functioning partly as a character and partly as an image, the raven at first appears comical and gradually grows sinister.

Sample Topics:

1. **Euphony:** This term refers to the harmonious combination of words. Discuss the euphony in Poe's work, how it is achieved, and how it affects your reading.

   To appreciate the extraordinary power of the sound of the poem, you must understand how Poe achieves it. This involves a close scrutiny of individual lines and phrases, as well as an acquaintance with such literary devices as assonance, consonance, and alliteration. An essay on this topic should describe both the methods and the effects. Although the meter and rhyme scheme remain constant throughout the poem, the feelings change markedly, from the gloomy but measured cadences of the opening to the wild shrieking at the end. You should also explain how these varied sounds fit the poem's changing action.

2. **The raven:** How does Poe use this image in the poem? How do your ideas about it change?

   The extraordinary image of the black bird seems to embody all the varied themes of the tale. It appears at first comical, even preposterous, and then seems to grow more demonic as the poem progresses. An essay could analyze how this effect is achieved. What words and ideas are attached to the bird at various points in the poem? At the same time, it is clear that it is the narrator, not the raven, who is changing. What does the calm passivity of the bird contribute to the action and ideas of the poem?

Compare and Contrast Essays

Essays in this category may focus on any aspect of the poem, from theme to style or diction. Begin by deciding what aspect of the poem you wish to explore. The choice of a work for comparison will follow from that.

Sample Topics:

1. **Comparing "The Philosophy of Composition" to "The Raven":**
   In an essay called "The Philosophy of Composition," Poe describes in detail the construction of "The Raven." Compare and contrast Poe's comments in the essay with the poem itself.

   Poe's essay purports to describe his actual methods in composing "The Raven," but readers may well doubt that his creative process was quite as mathematical as he claims. An essay could explain those parts of Poe's commentary that provide insight for readers of the poem. It would also be illuminating to reflect on the claims that seem fictional. What is it about the poem that makes the claims seem unlikely?

2. **Comparing "The Raven" to "Annabel Lee":** Both poems express the grief of speakers who have lost their loves. Discuss similarities and differences in the methods of these poems and the ideas they suggest.

   In addition to subject matter, the two poems share numerous other features, including their heavy reliance on meter and rhyme, their invocations of angels and demons, the suggestion of the increasing madness of their speakers, and more. It would be particularly interesting to explore the interrelationship of these shared features. When identifying differences, an essay should comment on how they result in different shades of meaning or effect.

3. **Comparing successive texts:** "The Raven" went through many revisions, spanning the course of years. What do these changes reveal about the poem's themes and methods?

   Examining successive versions of the poem opens a window on the poet's choices that can greatly enrich your reading. An essay would detail Poe's changes and discuss their effects. Which changes seem to shade meanings in a different way? Which clarify an idea? Which add ambiguity? Which seem to affect the sound of the poem more than the sense? Successive editions of "The Raven" are available on the Web site of the Edgar Allan Poe Society of Baltimore (http://www.eapoe.org).

4. **Comparing "The Raven" to "The Bells":** Discuss Poe's use of sound in these two poems.

Using this topic, you could analyze Poe's mastery of sound. Both poems are deeply rhythmic and melodic, beginning in one key and growing both gloomier and wilder. An essay could discuss both the how the sounds are created and how they are matched to the progression of ideas in each poem.

Bibliography for "The Raven"

Carlson, Eric W., ed. *The Recognition of Edgar Allan Poe: Selected Criticism since 1829.* Ann Arbor: U of Michigan P, 1970.

Person, Leland S. "Poe's Composition of Philosophy: Reading and Writing 'The Raven.'" *Arizona Quarterly* 46, no. 3 (Fall 1990): 1–15.

Poe, Edgar Allan. *Collected Poems of Edgar Allan Poe.* Ed. Thomas Ollive Mabbott. Cambridge, MA: Harvard UP, 1978.

———. "The Philosophy of Composition." *Poe: Essays and Reviews.* New York: Library of America, 1984. 13–25.

———. "The Poetic Principle." *Poe: Essays and Reviews.* New York: Library of America, 1984. 71–94.

———. "The Rationale of Verse." *Poe: Essays and Reviews.* New York: Library of America, 1984. 26–70.

Quinn, Arthur Hobson. *Edgar Allan Poe: A Critical Biography.* New York: Appleton-Century-Crofts, 1941.

Silverman, Kenneth. *Edgar A. Poe: Mournful and Never-Ending Remembrance.* New York: HarperCollins, 1991.

"ANNABEL LEE"

READING TO WRITE

"**A**NNABEL LEE" is the last poem Poe wrote and, next to "The Raven," his most popular. Like many of his tales, the poem offers two almost opposite interpretations. Many people read it as a lyrical portrait of eternal love, while others read it similarly to "The Raven" as tracing the psychological breakdown of its narrator.

Those in the first group focus their attention on the haunting beauty of the poem, especially in its description of youthful love. Readers who take a darker view note the anger that the speaker expresses, the bizarre behavior he describes at the end of the poem, and the manic explosion of rhyme in the final stanza.

Certainly all seems lovely at the start of the poem:

> It was many and many a year ago,
>   In a kingdom by the sea,
> That a maiden there lived whom you may know
>   By the name of Annabel Lee;—
> And this maiden she lived with no other thought
>   Than to love and be loved by me.

The opening lines and the setting prepare readers to hear a fairy tale romance. At this point, the rhythm and rhyme feel sweet and enchanting. The narrator's suggestion in stanzas 2 and 3 that the angels coveted the love between him and Annabel Lee seems charming, reminiscent of a child's being told that the angels needed his or her mother in heaven. The suggestion that the listener may have known Annabel Lee seems a bit odd, but not odd enough to break the spell.

By stanza 3 the feeling changes. Is this only because of the death of Annabel Lee? In stanza 4 the once-charming idea about the angels has morphed into a paranoid insistence that "all men know" that the angels killed Annabel out of sheer, miserable envy. The fifth stanza seems filled with resentment: directed glancingly at those older and wiser and then aimed sharply at the angels in heaven, who are compared to infernal demons bent on severing two souls joined in love. This anger can be read as a stage in the grieving process. The question for the reader is, Does the speaker pass beyond this stage to acceptance or spiral further down into madness?

At the end of the poem the speaker is sleeping in Annabel's tomb:

> For the moon never beams, without bringing me dreams
>   Of the beautiful Annabel Lee;
> And the stars never rise, but I feel the bright eyes
>   Of the beautiful Annabel Lee:—
> And so, all the night-tide, I lie down by the side
>   Of my darling—my darling—my life and my bride,
> In her sepulchre there by the sea—
>   In her tomb by the sounding sea.

Is the final image one of calm resolution or hideous derangement? Changes in the sound of the poem may offer a clue. The incessant repetition of the ending words "sea," "Lee," and "me" is now compounded by the addition of internal rhymes in the first and third lines of the stanza, followed by the twice-repeated rhyme in the fifth and sixth lines. Does this make the poem more lovely than ever, or has it moved from enchanting to insane? The rhythm, too, reaches here a new frenzy. Until now, two-syllable iambic feet have been mixed with three-syllable anapests, relieving somewhat the sing-song rhythm. But in the final stanza the iambs are banished, and the poem is locked by an inescapable string of anapests into a relentless race to the tomb by the sounding sea.

TOPICS AND STRATEGIES
Themes

Although the theme is the ideas that a work raises, in writing about theme in poetry, do not focus too narrowly on what the poem says. As the discussion in the previous section illustrates, it is important to consider all elements of a poem. In "Annabel Lee," especially, the sound of the poem and the way it changes may suggest ideas about its themes.

Sample Topics:

1. **Loss:** How does "Annabel Lee" present the idea of grief?

   Obviously, the poem expresses the mourner's pain, but how is the experience reflected in the poem's construction? How does the poem change from beginning to end? How might these changes suggest a progression in the feelings of the speaker? One of the stages of human grief is anger. Where does anger appear in the poem? At whom is it directed?

2. **Dreams:** In what ways is the poem dreamlike? What does it suggest about dreaming?

   An essay on this topic would identify the words that give the poem an unreal feeling. Does its lovely dreaminess mask its darkness? What might this suggest about the nature of dreaming?

3. **Madness:** Many readers believe that the poem traces the descent of a man from grief to madness.

   What words and ideas in the poem and what elements of form indicate changes in the speaker's feelings? In particular, how does the pattern of rhythm and rhyme become maddening to the reader? An essay might discuss what the poem suggests about the source of the man's madness or the path of his descent.

History and Context

Many readers reflexively connect the poem with the death of Poe's own wife. In fact, a number of other women known to Poe, including some whom he knew as a child, have been identified as possible originals for his lost love. It has also been suggested that the original for the speaker was not Poe but Rufus Griswold, an acquaintance and rival, who was known to have slept at his wife's tomb. Making connections between a poem and its real-life sources can be interesting and instructive, as long as you avoid certain pitfalls. Biographical information should be viewed as something like the raw material from which a poem is created, not as a record to be used to check the validity of interpretations.

Sample Topics:

1. **Biographical sources:** Discuss the poem in relation to its possible sources.

   As described immediately above, a body of speculation exists regarding possible originals for Annabel Lee and even the speaker. For information, you might consult T. O. Mabbott's collection of Poe's poems. Research into to real-life sources is best used as background to point you to ideas that you may then explore in the poem.

2. **Death:** Death at an early age was common in Poe's day, and sad tales of loss were a staple of poems and popular songs throughout the century. Discuss "Annabel Lee" in the context of this literature.

   An essay on this topic might begin by reviewing characteristics of such literature in Poe's time. Then you might examine Poe's poem in relation to these characteristics. In what ways is it similar? In what ways does it stand apart from or comment on this literature?

Form and Genre

It is difficult to resist the judgment that what is most memorable about "Annabel Lee" is the music it creates. If you are not familiar with prosody, it is worth studying the subject just to be able to analyze how Poe creates his spellbinding sound. Besides analyzing how he creates it, an essay could also explain the purposes to which he puts it—how it fits with the overall design of the poem.

Sample Topics:

1. **Versification:** Discuss Poe's use of rhythm and rhyme in the poem.

The "Reading to Write" section describes how the poem's use of repetition, rhythm, and rhyme helps create the sound of madness. Another possible topic is the poem's "prettiness." To what extent does the melody, as well as the diction, sugarcoat the poem and mask its horror?

2. **Poe's ideas about poetry:** Explain Poe's ideas about poetic composition as discussed in "The Poetic Principle," "The Philosophy of Composition," and "The Rationale of Verse" and discuss their application to "Annabel Lee."

Poe offered many guidelines for good poetry, some quite specific. He did not always feel obliged, however, to follow them in his own composition. An essay could examine some of Poe's ideas and discuss the extent to which they are, or are not, observable in "Annabel Lee."

Language, Symbols, and Imagery

"Annabel Lee" is a poem that benefits from close analysis of its word use and imagery. Images of sea, tomb, and angels are easy to identify. In writing about them, it is usually best to avoid reducing them to what they "mean." A better approach is to describe the ideas and feelings the images suggest; this process often involves careful analysis of how the image is deployed in the poem.

Sample Topics:

1. **Diction:** Describe the diction in the poem and how it contributes to the overall design.

An essay might discuss the striking simplicity of the diction. Poe's use of short, simple words and frequent repetition ("love and be loved," "we loved with a love that was more than love") gives the poem some of the flavor of a book for beginning readers. This diction suits the idea in the poem of the childlike simplicity of the lovers. As the poem progresses, does the cumulative effect of simple and repetitive diction convey a different feeling? As the ideas grow more somber, the narrator's diction seems increasingly inappropriate. Does this reveal him as a childlike innocent lost in a world of experience? Or is his unvarying diction a symptom of compulsion or separation from reality?

2. **The sea:** Discuss Poe's use of this image in the poem.

An essay could examine closely the appearance of the sea throughout the poem. How does the opening image of "a kingdom by the sea," which seems part of a fairy tale, contrast with the concluding image, in which the sea is paired with Annabel Lee's sepulchre? Between these two appearances, the phrase "this kingdom by the sea" is repeated five times in three stanzas, in some instances feeling rather forced. In the fifth stanza, the "kingdom" disappears, and the sea is paired with "demons." An essay could analyze these various appearances and the ideas and feelings they engender.

Compare and Contrast Essays

"Annabel Lee" stands out as an exceptional poem on a very common theme. A good essay topic would be to identify what makes the poem so extraordinary and compare the poem to another. Poems about lost loves abound. Many popular songs take up the subject as well. Any of these might be used for comparison.

Sample Topics:

1. **Comparing "Annabel Lee" to possible source poems:** Two poems have been identified that may have influenced Poe in the writing of "Annabel Lee." Discuss Poe's poem in relation to either or both of these possible sources.

These poems are printed in T. O. Mabbot's anthology of Poe's poetry. One, "The Mourner," by an unknown author, is strikingly similar to "Annabel Lee." A comparison with this poem could point to many of the features of Poe's poem that set it so far above the ordinary. The second, "Stanzas for Music," by Sarah Helen Whitman, resembles "Annabel Lee" less closely, but was written by a friend of Poe's. You might consider "Annabel Lee" as a kind of response.

2. **Comparing "Annabel Lee" and "The Raven":** Both poems express the grief of speakers who have lost their loves. Discuss similarities and differences in the methods of these poems and the ideas they suggest.

This topic is discussed in the "Compare and Contrast" section of the chapter on "The Raven." You might also review the question suggesting a comparison between "The Raven" and "The Bells." The latter poem might also be compared with "Annabel Lee."

Bibliography for "Annabel Lee"

Carlson, Eric W., ed. *The Recognition of Edgar Allan Poe. Selected Criticism since 1829.* Ann Arbor: U of Michigan P, 1970.

Dayan, Joan. "Amorous Bondage: Poe, Ladies and Slaves." *The American Face of Edgar Allan Poe.* Ed. Shawn Rosenheim and Stephen Rachman. Baltimore: Johns Hopkins UP, 1995. 179–209.

Kennedy, J. Gerald. *Poe, Death, and the Life of Writing.* New Haven, CT: Yale UP, 1987.

Poe, Edgar Allan. *Collected Poems of Edgar Allan Poe.* Ed. Thomas Ollive Mabbott. Cambridge, MA: Harvard UP, 1978.

Quinn, Arthur Hobson. *Edgar Allan Poe: A Critical Biography.* New York: Appleton-Century-Crofts, 1941.

Silverman, Kenneth. *Edgar A. Poe: Mournful and Never-Ending Remembrance.* New York: HarperCollins, 1991.

Stovall, Floyd. *Edgar Poe the Poet: Essays New and Old on the Man and His Work.* Charlottesville: UP of Virginia, 1969.

Wilbur, Richard. "Poe and the Art of Suggestion." *Critical Essays on Edgar Allan Poe.* Ed. Eric W. Carlson. New York: G. K. Hall and Company, 1987. 160–71.

INDEX

HUBBARD HIGH SCHOOL LIBRARY
6200 South Hamlin Avenue
Chicago, Illinois 60629